MASTERING THE IPHONE 15:

A Comprehensive Guide for Beginners
and Experts on how to use your iPhone 15,
iPhone Pro, and 15 Promax

Edward M. Davis

TABLE OF CONTENT

CONCLUSION

INTRODUCTION

Welcome to the world of the iPhone 15, iPhone Pro, and 15 Promax—an ecosystem that reimagines how we connect, create, and communicate via the seamless fusion of creativity and technology. With the help of "Mastering the iPhone 15: A Comprehensive Guide for Beginners and Experts," take a trip through the most recent products from Apple and gain the skills necessary to utilize your device to the fullest.

Regardless of your level of computer expertise or level of familiarity with the iPhone, this extensive guide is meant to be your reliable friend. Every chapter is designed to provide users of all skill levels more power, from the basic setup to the unearthing of complex capabilities. Learn about the subtleties of the upgraded camera system, make use of Siri's skills, and investigate the state-of-the-art augmented reality features available on the iPhone 15 series.

Beyond the fundamentals, discover performance-boosting optimization strategies, become familiar with iCloud's complexities, and personalize your iPhone to your tastes. Diagnose typical problems, investigate professional advice, and be ahead of the curve with predictions about upcoming developments and trends.

This book is an investigation of possibilities rather than just a guide. Discover hidden functions, become proficient with complex settings, and realize your iPhone's full potential. Mastering the iPhone 15 is your go-to guide whether you're using the newest technology to keep ahead of the curve, communicate with ease, or take amazing pictures.

Come along as we delve into the details of the iPhone 15 series, giving you the know-how and resources to

completely change the way you interact with iPhones.
Let's go on our journey!

CHAPTER 1: GETTING STARTED

To begin using your iPhone 15, iPhone Pro, or 15 Pro Max, follow these steps:

1. Opening:

   You will find your iPhone, a pair of earphones, a charging cable, and maybe a power converter when you first open the package. Examine the contents for a moment to make sure everything is there.

2. Activate:

   Holding down the side or home button will cause the Apple logo to show. Set up your device by following the directions on the screen.

3. Join a Wi-Fi network:

   Select the WiFi network of your choice, then type in the password. This is necessary to access different internet functions, set up iCloud, and download updates.

4. Configure Face ID or Touch ID:

For increased security and convenience, configure Touch ID or Face ID, depending on the model. Making sure that only you can unlock your iPhone requires this step.

5. Optional Backup Restoration:

During the setup process, if you're upgrading from an older iPhone, you can restore your data from an iTunes or iCloud backup.

6. iCloud and Apple ID:

Use your Apple ID to log in, or create a new one. iCloud offers backup capabilities and data syncing between devices.

7. Set Up Siri: Tailor Siri's preferences and teach it to identify your voice. Siri can help with a variety of chores and improve the effectiveness of your iPhone experience.

8. Enable Find My: If your cell phone is lost or stolen, turn on the "Find my iPhone" feature. This can be completed in the Settings app later on or during setup.

9. Look around the App Store:

Get your preferred applications by visiting the App Store. To improve the capabilities of your iPhone, you can also investigate new ones.

10. Adjust Configurations:

To customize the experience of your iPhone, open the Settings app. You can customize the display, noises, notifications, and more to suit your tastes.

11. Upgrade Software:

On your iPhone, make sure the most recent version of iOS is installed. To find and install any available updates, navigate to Settings > General > Software Update.

12. Discover New Features: Become acquainted with the latest features, such as camera improvements, display

technologies, and any exclusive capabilities, of your particular iPhone model.

13. Protect Your Device: To provide extra protection, set up a password or passcode. These settings are located in the Settings app's Face ID & Passcode or Touch ID & Passcode sections.

14. Take Pleasure in Your iPhone:

You can now use and configure your iPhone. Make use of the newest technology, explore its capabilities, and get the most out of your new gadget.

1:1 Setting Up Your iPhone

It's simple to set up your iPhone 15, iPhone Pro, or iPhone 15 Pro Max. Here's a comprehensive how-to to get you going:

1. Unboxing: Examine the contents of your iPhone after carefully opening the package. Make sure you have the charging cable, earbuds, iPhone, and any other accessories that come with it.

2. Turn on the power: Press and hold the home or side buttons to see the Apple logo. Start the setup procedure by following the directions on the screen.

3. Language and location: Select the language and location that you want to use. This option establishes the region-based settings and chooses the language for the iPhone's user interface.

4. Optional Quick Start: You may use the Quick Start feature on an older iPhone running iOS 11 or later. To transfer data, just put the old and new iPhones next to each other and follow the on-screen instructions.

5. Enable Wi-Fi: After choosing your Wi-Fi network, type the password in. To finish the setup, update the device, and use other functions, you need to have an active Wi-Fi connection.

6. Configure Face ID or Touch ID: Choose between Touch ID and Face ID depending on the model of your iPhone. Your device's security and privacy are improved by these biometric security measures.

7. Backup Restore (Optional):
   Throughout the setup process, you can restore your data, applications, and settings from an earlier iPhone backup that is stored in iCloud or iTunes.

8. iCloud and Apple ID: Use your Apple ID to log in, or create a new one. To use the App Store, iCloud services, and other Apple features, you must have your Apple ID.

9. Customize Your Settings: You may add personality to your iPhone by adjusting settings like Wallpaper, Sounds and haptics, and Display and brightness. These are modifiable to your personal preference.

10. Siri Setup: To teach Siri to recognize your voice, turn on Siri and follow the instructions. Siri can help you with tasks, provide answers to your queries, and operate other iPhone functionalities.

11. Turn on Find My: For security reasons, turn on the "Find My iPhone" feature. If your smartphone is lost or stolen, this aids in its location. Settings > [your name] > Discover My > Find My iPhone is where you may discover this setting.

12. Optionally Set Up Apple Pay: Add your credit or debit cards to the Wallet app to utilize Apple Pay. This allows you to use your iPhone to make safe payments.

13. Look Around in the App Store: To download and install your preferred apps, go to the App Store. You can improve your iPhone experience by exploring categories, finding new apps, and searching for certain ones.

14. Update Software: Look for and apply any available software updates. Navigate to Software Update under Settings > General. Updating the software on your iPhone guarantees security and optimal performance.

15. Configure a password or passcode: Establishing a passcode or password will improve security. To set up these security measures, open the Settings app and navigate to Face ID & Passcode or Touch ID & Passcode.

16. Appreciate Your iPhone: You can now use and configure your iPhone. Examine its functions, try out its

gestures, and relish having the newest technology at your disposal.

1:2 Navigating the Home Screen

With your iPhone 15, iPhone Pro, or 15 Pro Max, navigating the Home Screen is simple and easy. This article will assist you in comprehending and optimizing your Home Screen:

1. Unlocking Your iPhone: Depending on the features of your smartphone, you can use Face ID, Touch ID, or your passcode to unlock your iPhone and get to the Home Screen.

2. Layout of Home Screen: Apps and widgets are located on the Home Screen. Icons are used to symbolize apps, which you can organize by moving them to various screens or organizing them into folders.

3. Icons for Applications: To open an app, tap its icon once. To access the edit mode, press and hold an icon until it begins to jitter. This gives you the ability to

reorganize your Home Screen, make folders, and move or remove apps.

4. Notification Center and Control Center: For quick settings and shortcuts, swipe down from the upper-right corner of the screen to open the Control Center. To view notifications and widgets in the Notification Center, swipe down from the top of the screen.

5. Application Library: To access the App Library, which automatically groups your apps into categories, swipe right on the Home Screen. To find and open apps, use the search box or navigate through the categories.

6. Customizing Widgets: Widgets offer information that is easily viewed. Press and hold an empty area on the Home Screen, tap the '+' symbol in the upper-left corner, then choose the widgets you wish to add. This allows you to add or modify widgets.

7. Building Files: Drag an app icon onto another to create a folder and organize your apps that way. The

folder can then be renamed, and further apps can be added. Folders facilitate app discovery and help keep your Home Screen organized.

8. Changing Wallpaper: You can customize your Home Screen by altering the background image. Grab and hold an empty area, select "Wallpaper," and select a different background. You can use your images or choose from the wallpapers that Apple has provided.

9. Search the App Library: To quickly access apps, use the App Library's search box. Once you begin typing the name of the app, the App Library will filter and show appropriate results.

10. Movements: Learn how to use simple motions like pinching inward to zoom out and see all of your Home Screen pages, swiping up from the bottom to access the App Switcher, and swiping left or right to switch between Home Screen pages.

11. Lock: Your Home Screen's bottom row of icons is called the Dock. Your most utilized apps should go in this section, which is accessible from any Home Screen page.

12. App Library Organization: Your apps are cleverly categorized by the App Library. Examine these categories, then press any of them to open apps off of your Home Screen.

You can manage your iPhone fast and efficiently if you become familiar with these Home Screen functions and motions. You are welcome to personalize your iPhone experience by customizing your Home Screen to fit your tastes.

1:3 Configuring Basic Settings

You may customize your iPhone 15, iPhone Pro, or 15 Pro Max to your liking by configuring its basic settings. Here's a tutorial to assist you in configuring basic options:

1. Getting to the Settings: You can access the Settings app by clicking on the gear icon located on your Home Screen. This is where you go to change all the different settings for your iPhone.

2. Wi-Fi: Open the Settings app and choose the Wi-Fi option to establish a connection. For quicker data access and software upgrades, select your network, type in the password, and make sure your internet connection is steady.

3. Bluetooth: To link your iPhone to other gadgets like speakers, headphones, or your car's music system, turn on Bluetooth in the Settings.

4. Cellular Data: Go to Settings > Cellular to keep an eye on and manage your consumption of cellular data. You can monitor your total data usage and allow or stop cellular data for particular apps.

5. Personal Hotspot: Create a Personal Hotspot in the Cellular section of Settings to allow you to share your iPhone's internet connection with other devices. When you need to utilize your laptop or tablet to access the internet, this is helpful.

6. Notifications: Modify app alerts using the Notifications area. You have control over which apps can notify you, how they look on the lock screen, and which alert styles they can use.

7. Display & Brightness: Select your desired display settings, adjust the brightness, and turn on or off True Tone in this section. Night Shift can also be set up to minimize exposure to blue light in the evening.

8. Audio & Touch: Change the text tone, ringtone, and other audio preferences in Sounds & Haptics. You can change the sound settings, including volume and vibration on/off.

9. Touch ID or Face ID:

Set up or adjust the biometric security features on your device under the Face ID & Passcode or Touch ID & Passcode area. This makes unlocking your iPhone easier and strengthens its security.

10. Do Not Disturb: Activate Do Not Disturb to turn off notifications, calls, and messages at particular times. This option is included in the Settings app's Do Not Disturb section.

11. Overall Configurations: To access a variety of device-wide adjustments, navigate to the General area of Settings. This covers VPN settings, background app refreshes, software upgrades, and more.

12. Background App Refresh: Select if background content refreshes are possible for apps. This can be adjusted in the General settings, Background App Refresh section.

13. Privacy Settings: Examine and control the privacy settings you have set. To limit an app's access to features like contacts, the camera, and location services, go to Settings > Privacy.

14. Search & Siri: In the Siri & Search menu, adjust the Siri settings. You can control which apps can utilize Siri, enable Siri suggestions, and modify voice feedback.

15. App Store Settings: Adjust the App Store's settings, including those for in-app purchases and automatic downloads. These settings are located in the Settings app store section.

16. Updated Software: Ensure that the iOS version on your iPhone is the most recent one. Examine the software update by going to Settings > General >

Software Update. Updating your gadget guarantees better security and performance.

You may customize your iPhone to your tastes and improve your overall experience by going through these fundamental options. Make sure your device is operating effectively and securely by checking and updating these settings regularly.

CHAPTER 2: MASTERING THE BASICS

Gaining a thorough understanding of the fundamentals of your iPhone 15, iPhone Pro, or 15 Pro Max is necessary for a smooth and effective user experience. Three key points to consider are as follows:

1. Understanding Gestures:
 - Swipe Up: To unlock your device or go back to the Home Screen from an app.

 - Swipe Down: From the top-right and top-middle, respectively, access the Control Center and Notification Center.

 - To navigate between multiple Home Screen pages, Swipe Left or Right.

- Pinch In or Out: Extend and contract the zoom on images and webpages.

- Swipe Between Apps: To move between recently used apps, swipe left or right at the bottom of the screen.

2. Managing Notifications:
 - Notification Center: To access widgets and notifications, swipe down from the top of the screen. You can choose which widgets show up and in what sequence.

-Clearing Notifications: Swipe left on notifications to dismiss them, then press "Clear" or "Clear All" to clear them all.

- Customizing Notifications for Apps: Select Notifications under Settings to customize how each app notifies you. Notification styles, sounds, and whether or not they show up on the lock screen are all customizable.

- Do Not Disturb: To block calls and notifications during particular times, use the Control Center or Settings app's Do Not Disturb function.

3. Making the most of the Control Center:
- Getting to the Control Center: Drag down from the upper-right position. Swipe up from the bottom on iPhone models that include a Home button.

- Control Center Customization: To change the order of, add, or remove shortcuts, navigate to Settings > Control Center. Toggles for brightness, Bluetooth, Wi-Fi, and other features are included.

- Quick Actions: To access more options, 3D Touch or long-press Control Center shortcuts. For instance, you can adjust the brightness by 3D Touching the flashlight symbol.

Your experience with the iPhone will be much improved by learning these fundamentals. You'll be able to use the Control Center, handle notifications, and operate your iPhone with ease and efficiency as you get more comfortable with these movements. As you continue to explore the features and settings on your device, feel free to try out more settings.

2:1 Making and Receiving Calls

One essential feature of your iPhone 15, iPhone Pro, or 15 Pro Max is the ability to make and receive calls. Here's a how-to tutorial for doing it successfully:

Placing Calls:

1. Phone App:
 - Tap the Phone app after finding it on your Home Screen.
   - At the bottom of the screen, you'll see tabs for Voicemail, Contacts, Recents, and Favorites.

2. Pressing the Number:
   - Press the symbol of the keypad located at the bottom of the screen.
   - Enter the phone number using the keypad.

3. Using Contacts to Place a Call:
   - In the Phone app, tap the Contacts tab.

- Locate and tap the name of the person you wish to call.

   - Press the symbol for a phone by their number.

4. Calling One of Your Favorites:
   - Take a tap at the Favorites tab in the Phone app.
   - Select the Favorites tab in the Phone app.

5. FaceTime Calls:
   - Use FaceTime for video calls. Start a FaceTime call straight from the Contacts app, or open the FaceTime app.

6. Using Siri:
   - Press and hold the side or home button to bring up Siri, then type "Call [contact name]" or "Call [phone number]."

Getting Phone Calls:

1. Answering a Call:

- The caller's name or number appears on the screen when you get a call.

- Slide to the right and tap the green phone icon to respond.

2. Rejecting a Call:

- Press the red phone icon to reject a call. Additionally, you can put the call on hold by pressing the side or home button once, or twice to send it to voicemail.

3. Respond with a Message:

- If you are unable to answer, you may either generate a personalized message under Settings > Phone > Respond with Text, or you can respond quickly by hitting the message button.

4. Decline with Reminders:

- Select a time and touch "Remind Me" to set a reminder to call you back.

5. Siling Incoming Calls:

- Press the volume buttons, side or home buttons, or both to end an incoming call.

6. Sending and receiving FaceTime calls:
- You will be given the choice to accept or reject a FaceTime call when it is received. To access more choices, such as messaging someone or creating a reminder, swipe up.

7. Emergency SOS: - To activate Emergency SOS, rapidly press the side or home button five times. This can automatically dial 911.

Make sure that call waiting, call forwarding, and other settings are set up to suit your needs by checking your mobile device's and FaceTime settings. Comprehending these fundamentals will enable you to make and receive calls on your iPhone with assurance.

2:2 Sending Texts and Multimedia Messages

It's simple and usual to send SMS and multimedia messages (pictures and videos) on your iPhone 15, iPhone Pro, or iPhone 15 Pro Max. Here's a tutorial on sending several kinds of messages:

Texting Others (SMS):

1. Messages App:
 - Click the green icon with the white speech bubble to open the Messages app.

2. Start a New Message:
 - To begin a new message, tap the compose icon (pencil) in the upper-right corner.

3. Please enter the recipient.
-Insert the recipient's name or phone number in the To: field. To choose a contact from your list, you can alternatively hit the '+' icon.

4. Write Your Note:

 - Press the text area and begin writing your note.

5. Send:

 - To send your text message, click the blue send arrow.

Multimedia Messaging Service (MMS) Sending:

1. Follow the Above Steps 1-3:

 - Launch the Messages app, select New, and enter the recipient's details.

2. Please Attach Media: Tap the camera icon next to the text area to send a picture or a video. Choose an image or video from your collection, or take a fresh one.

3. Send Media:

 - To send the multimedia message, click the blue send arrow after attaching the media.

With iMessage:

1. Enable iMessage:

- Make sure that Messages > Settings > iMessage is enabled. With iMessage, you can communicate with other Apple devices via text messages, images, videos, and more via Wi-Fi or cellular connection.

2. Features of iMessage:

- You can send animated stickers, reactions, and other multimedia files over iMessage.

- Regular SMS messages appear in green bubbles, but iMessage communications sent between Apple devices are displayed in blue bubbles.

Notes for the Group:

1. Create a Group:

- In the Messages app, create a group to send a message to several recipients.

2. Add Contacts:

- Type your message, add recipients, and begin a new conversation. The message will be displayed to all recipients, and responses will be available to all group members.

With Siri:

1. Start Siri:
- You can send texts hands-free with Siri. Holding down the home or side buttons will activate Siri. Say, Send a message to [contact name].

2. Dictate Message:
– You will be prompted by Siri to narrate your message. Siri will confirm when you're done, at which point you can send the message.

It's important to monitor your Wi-Fi or cellular data usage, particularly when sending multimedia communications, as these can consume bandwidth. You may use your iPhone to send text and multimedia messages more efficiently if you follow these instructions.

2:3 Managing Contacts

Keeping your contacts on your iPhone 15, iPhone Pro, or 15 Pro Max organized and easily accessible is essential. Here's a how-to for efficiently managing and arranging your contacts:

1. Introductory Data:
   - Click on your home screen and open the Contacts app.
   - To add a new contact, tap the '+' icon located in the upper-right corner.
   - Add the contact's email address, phone number, and any other relevant information.
   - To attach a photo to the contact, tap "Add Photo".

2. Importing Contacts:
   - You can import contacts if you're moving from one device to another. Use third-party programs like iCloud

or Google Contacts, or navigate to Settings > Contacts > Import SIM Contacts.

3. Making Changes to Contacts:

 - Open the Contacts app, choose a contact, and then press "Edit" in the upper-right corner to make changes to that contact.

 - If necessary, update the contact information, then hit "Done" to save the modifications.

4. Organizing Contacts:

 - Create contact groups to organize contacts. In the Contacts app, tap "Groups" and choose "New Group." Organize groups more easily by adding contacts.

5. Contacts to be Removed:

- Open the Contacts app, choose the contact to remove, and then select "Edit."

 - After swiping down, select "Delete Contact." Verify the removal.

6. Combine Identical Contacts:

- Go to Settings > Contacts > Find & Merge Contacts to see if you have any duplicate contacts. This function aids in organizing your contact list.

7. Partnership Contacts:
- A contact can be shared by opening the Contacts app, choosing it, and then tapping "Share Contact." Select the preferred method for sending the contact details: email, AirDrop, or messaging.

8. Using iCloud for Contacts:
- Go to Settings > [your name] > iCloud and turn on iCloud Contacts. By doing this, all of your Apple devices' contacts are synchronized.

9. Exporting Contacts:
- Make a backup of your contacts using iCloud or other third-party apps before exporting them. When switching between devices, this can be helpful.

10. Backup Contacts:

- To prevent data loss, regularly back up your contacts. iTunes and iCloud can assist with this.

11. Managing Contact Information:
- To get a complete picture of your connections, add specific details to contacts, like birthdays, addresses, and remarks.

12. Using Siri for Contacts:
- Turn Siri on and instruct her to message or phone a contact. Additionally, Siri can assist you in finding contact details quickly.

13. Contact Search:
- To locate particular contacts fast, use the Contacts app's search box. You can conduct a phone number, email, or name search.

14. Export Contacts to Third-Party Apps:
– Some customers would rather use apps from third parties to handle their contacts. Look through the App

Store's choices to add more features and customize your experience.

You may effectively manage and arrange your contacts by following these steps, which will make it easy for you to get in touch with the individuals who are most important to you. Keeping your contacts organized and updated regularly will make communicating on your iPhone easier.

CHAPTER 3: EXPLORING THE FEATURES

By exploring its features, you can get the most out of your iPhone 15, iPhone Pro, or 15 Pro Max, giving you a customized and effective user experience. Here's a guide to help you explore and learn about the wide range of features at your disposal:

1. Customization of the Control Center:
 - To reach the Control Center, swipe down from the upper-right corner. You can customize it by 3D touching or long-pressing icons to get more possibilities. Shortcuts can be added or removed to provide easy access to key functions.

 2. Home Screen Widgets:
 - Long-press the home screen, select the "+" symbol, and add widgets to display information quickly. Widgets show the most recent information from your preferred apps and are available in multiple sizes.

3. Exploring the App Library:

- To reach the App Library, where apps are automatically categorized, swipe left on the home screen. To locate any app quickly, tap the search box at the top.

4. Live Text in Photos:

- Use Live Text in the Photos app to interact with the text within your photos. You may instantly copy, paste, look up, or translate text from your photos.

5. Focus Modes:

- Customize Focus modes to filter alerts according to where you are or what you're doing. Navigate to Settings > Focus to access this function and customize it to fit different parts of your day.

6. Quick Note Creation:

- To make a Quick Note, swipe with your finger or the Apple Pencil from the bottom-right corner of the screen. These notes sync across all of your Apple devices and are readily accessible.

7. Notification Summary:

- Receive grouped notifications at particular times by customizing your Notification Summary. Go to Settings > Focus > Notification Summary to control this feature.

8. AirPods Integration:

- Dynamic head tracking, conversation boost, and spatial audio experiences are made possible by the seamless integration with AirPods. Navigate to Settings > Bluetooth > (Your AirPods) to explore these features.

9. Text Recognition in Photos:

- To identify and highlight text in real-time, utilize the text recognition capability of the Camera app. This is very helpful when taking notes from documents or signage.

10. Interactive Maps:

- Discover dynamic 3D maps and in-depth city experiences with Apple Maps. Take a helicopter tour over cities and explore fully immersive augmented reality navigation.

11. Hidden Shazam Integration:

- The Control Center has Shazam integrated. Tap the Shazam icon to identify music without opening a separate app.

12. Application Videos:

- Use App Clips to quickly access particular app features without having to download the entire app. To start these mini-app experiences, utilize NFC tags or scan App Clip codes.

13. Improved Safari Encounter:

- Safari provides a revamped online experience. Utilize grouped tabs, the bottom tab bar for navigation, and the simplified address bar.

14. Private Relay in iCloud+:

- Learn about iCloud+'s privacy-focused features, such as Private Relay. This function assists in protecting your online privacy and connection security while you browse.

15. Health App Overview:

- Explore the Health app to get in-depth knowledge about fitness and health. Track trends, get health advice, and experiment with new features like Walking Steadiness.

16. Updates for CarPlay:

- Check out the revised CarPlay UI, which includes better Maps and support for additional app categories, if you use it. Savor a more smooth and user-friendly driving experience.

17. Siri Enhancements:

- Siri keeps becoming better at contextual comprehension and natural language processing. Try out tailored responses and hands-free commands.

18. Advanced Face ID and Touch ID:

- To improve accuracy and security, Face ID and Touch ID have been improved. Get quicker authentication and unlocking for all of your apps and services.

19. Camera Styles:

- Create and modify your photo styles right within the Camera app. To get pictures that suit your style, play around with the tone and warmth settings.

20. The Updated Weather App:

- The Weather app has an eye-catching, educational design. For an immersive experience, investigate maps, dynamic backgrounds, and weather conditions.

By exploring these options, you may customize your iPhone experience and take full use of the cutting-edge technologies made to improve your day-to-day living. You'll learn about the depth and adaptability of your iPhone 15 series smartphone as you work your way through these features.

3:1 Face ID and Touch ID

The biometric authentication capabilities on iPhones, Face ID, and Touch ID, improve device security and offer easy ways to unlock your phone, make transactions, and authenticate different apps. Below is a summary of each:

Face Recognition:

1. Introduction:
- Newer iPhones, such as the iPhone X and later models, that do not have a physical home button can use Face ID.
   - It authenticates different transactions and securely unlocks your iPhone using facial recognition technology.

2. Enabling Face ID:
- You can enroll in Face ID in Settings at any time after your iPhone is first set up. To enable the TrueDepth

camera to capture various facial angles, the setup entails rotating your face in a circular motion.

3. Unlocking Your iPhone:
 - To wake your iPhone, just lift it or press the screen.
   - When Face ID detects your face, your device's lock icon unlocks, giving you access.

4. Securing Payments and Apps:
- Face ID may be used to authorize Apple Pay transactions, secure sensitive data within apps, and authenticate app logins.

5. Attention Awareness:
- Before the smartphone opens, Face ID makes sure that your eyes are open and focused on it.

6. Security Measures:
 - Only a mathematical representation of your face is utilized for authentication, and Face ID data is safely kept in the device's Secure Enclave.

- It continuously adjusts to aesthetic changes over time, such as the development of facial hair or the need for glasses.

Touch ID:

Introduction: - Touch ID is compatible with iPhones that have a physical home button, such as the iPhone 5s, iPhone 8, and some iPad models.
   - To verify users, a fingerprint sensor integrated into the home button is used.

2. Enabling Touch ID:
 - You can enroll your fingerprints by repeatedly pressing the home button on your smartphone during setup or afterward in Settings.

3. How to Unlock Your iPhone:
 - To unlock the smartphone, touch the home button and use a registered fingerprint.

4. Securing Payments and Apps:

- Touch ID may be used to authorize app purchases, authenticate Apple Pay transactions, and secure specific apps.

5. Numerous Fingerprints:
- You have the option to register numerous fingerprints, making it possible to authenticate transactions or unlock the device using different fingers.

6. Security Measures:
- Only a mathematical model of your fingerprint is utilized for authentication, and Touch ID data is also kept in the Secure Enclave.

Selecting Between Touch ID and Face ID:

Compatibility with Devices:
- The iPhone model you own will determine which of the two capabilities you can use: Face ID or Touch ID. Not all iPhone models support both.

Self-Preferred Style:

- While some users would like Touch ID's familiarity, others could favor Face ID's ease. Often, it boils down to personal taste.

Biometric Effectiveness:
 - Touch ID and Face ID are both very dependable and safe. Whichever approach best suits your usage habits and level of comfort will be the one you choose.

Whether you use Touch ID or Face ID, these biometric authentication techniques offer a seamless user experience and a safe and easy way to connect with your iPhone.

3-2 Siri and Voice Commands

With Apple's virtual assistant, Siri, you may use voice commands in natural language to communicate with your iPhone. It can answer questions, carry out a variety of tasks, and operate your device without your assistance. An introduction to Siri and voice commands is provided here:

Turning on Siri:

1. Voice instruction:
 - Say "Hey Siri" and then provide your instruction to activate Siri. On newer smartphones, you may also hold down the side or home button.

2. Setup "Hey Siri":
 - You can activate the "Listen for 'Hey Siri'" option under Settings > Siri & Search. This lets you use just your voice to launch Siri.

Using Siri to Issue Basic Input:

1. Telephoning and Messaging:
  - For instance: "Hey Siri, call John" instead of "Hey Siri, send a message to Sarah."

2. Alerting and Setting Reminders:
  - For instance: "Hey Siri, set a reminder for 3 PM" as well as "Hey Siri, set an alarm for 7 AM tomorrow."

3. Reviewing Data and Weather:
  - For instance, "Hey Siri, what's the weather today?" and "Hey Siri, tell me about the Eiffel Tower."

4. Opening Apps:
  - For instance, "Hey Siri, open Spotify" or "Hey Siri, open Maps."

Complex Siri Inputs:

1. Home Automation:

- Siri is capable of controlling smart home appliances. An illustration would be, "Hey Siri, turn off the lights."

2. Calculations and Conversions:
 - "Hey Siri, what's 25% of 150?" or even "Hey Siri, convert 5 miles to kilometers."

3. Language Translation:
 – Translations can be assisted by Siri. For instance, "Hey Siri, translate 'hello' to Spanish."

4. Getting Directions:
 - For instance, "Hey Siri, how do I get to the nearest gas station?"

 Siri Shortcuts:

1. Personalized Orders:
 - With Siri Shortcuts, you may program unique voice instructions for particular tasks or combinations of tasks.

2. Automation:

- You can make a shortcut that, for instance, launches your workout playlist, turns on Do Not Disturb, and sends a pre-written message to a particular contact.

Voice Command Hints:

1. Speak Naturally:
 - Siri can understand normal language, so you don't need to use special terms.

2. Correcting Siri:
- You can say, "Hey Siri, that's not what I asked," or offer a correction if Siri misinterprets or gives you incorrect information.

3. Voice Feedback:
 - Depending on your preference, Siri can either respond vocally or visually. This is configurable under Settings > Siri & Search.

4. Respecting Privacy:

- Siri uses the device's microphone to process spoken commands in private. Siri recordings are not saved by Apple unless you specifically choose to share them to enhance Siri's functionality.

With each new iOS release, Siri gains new features and enhances its comprehension of spoken language. Try out various voice command combinations to see what all your iPhone can do with Siri's help.

3:3 Augmented Reality on iPhone 15

Apple's most recent smartphone, the iPhone 15, represents a major advancement in augmented reality (AR) technology. The iPhone 15 blurs the boundaries between the real and virtual worlds by enhancing augmented reality experiences with its cutting-edge hardware and software.

ARKit 5: The Basis for Better Augmented Reality Experiences

ARKit 5, Apple's next-generation AR framework, is the brains behind the iPhone 15's augmented reality capabilities. With the introduction of several improvements, ARKit 5 enables developers to produce even more engaging and interactive augmented reality experiences.

Improved Object Monitoring:

With ARKit 5, object tracking is much enhanced, making it possible to follow real-world objects more steadily and accurately. Because of this, experiences using AR objects can be more realistic and captivating by blending in perfectly with the real environment.

Scene Perception:

With the introduction of scene understanding by ARKit 5, the iPhone 15 is now able to recognize surfaces, planes, and lighting conditions by analyzing its surroundings. By using this data, AR experiences can be made more realistic by precisely positioning things.

Spatial Fixtures:

With the addition of location anchors in ARKit 5, developers can now create augmented reality experiences that are both persistent and location-specific. This implies that even if the location of their iPhone has moved, consumers can return to the same spot for future AR experiences.

RealityKit: AR App Building Blocks:

Apple's high-level AR framework, RealityKit, enhances ARKit 5 by giving developers a robust toolkit for creating AR applications. RealityKit makes it easier for developers to realize their AR dreams by streamlining the process of producing augmented reality experiences.

Intelligent Coordination through Common Areas:

With shared areas, RealityKit facilitates real-time collaboration and allows several users to participate in the same augmented reality experience at the same time. This creates opportunities for cooperative AR experiences in industries like gaming, design, and education.

Improved Sound and Touch:

The improved haptic and audio features of the iPhone 15 improve augmented reality experiences even further.

Users can hear AR items as if they were there by using spatial audio, which gives them a sense of directionality. By giving tactile sensations that enhance the interaction with AR objects, haptic feedback enhances the immersion experience even more.

iPhone 15: An Opening to the Real Reality

The ever-expanding world of augmented reality is made accessible to users of the iPhone 15 thanks to its potent hardware, cutting-edge software, and unique features. ARKit 5 and RealityKit have the potential to build ground-breaking augmented reality experiences that will revolutionize a variety of spheres of our lives, including education, entertainment, healthcare, and design. Developers are already investigating this potential.

The iPhone 15 will continue to be at the vanguard of AR technology, enabling people to see the world in entirely new ways as it develops. There are countless options, and augmented reality has a bright future ahead of it.

CHAPTER 4: OPTIMIZING PERFORMANCE

Whether you have an iPhone 15, Pro, or 15 Pro Max, optimizing performance is essential to maintaining responsiveness and seamless operation. The following are some pointers to improve and preserve your device's performance:

1. Keep Software Updated:
 - Make sure to install iOS updates regularly. Bug fixes, security upgrades, and performance gains are frequently included in these updates.

2. Control Storage:
 - Pay attention to the storage on your device.
Performance may be impacted by full storage. Eliminate superfluous apps, images, and videos. To have programs that you don't often use automatically removed, use the "Offload Unused Apps" function in Settings.

3. Background App Refresh:

- to minimize background processes. For programs that don't require frequent updates, disable Background App Refresh by going to Settings > General > Background App Refresh.

4. Reduce Motion and Transparency:

- To reduce animations, activate "Reduce Motion" under Settings > Accessibility > Motion. Moreover, less transparency under Settings > Accessibility > Display & Text Size. Performance on older devices may be improved by this.

5. Manage Widgets:

- Take out of the Today View any widgets that aren't necessary. To access the Today View, swipe right on your Home Screen, then scroll down and select "Edit" to modify widgets.

6. Clear Safari Cache:

- Frequently clear the cache in your Safari browser. Navigate to Settings > Safari > Delete Website Data and History.

7. Limit App Refresh in the Background:
- Selectively enable App Background Refresh only for apps that require real-time updates by going to Settings > General > App Background Refresh.

8. Restart Your iPhone:
- To clear temporary files and update system processes, restart your iPhone regularly. This can help fix small bugs and enhance functionality in general.

9. Check Battery Health:
- Check your battery's maximum capacity via Settings > Battery > Battery Health. For best results, replace the battery if it has considerably deteriorated.

10. Turn off dynamic wallpapers:

- Dynamic wallpapers have the potential to use more resources. Use static wallpapers in its place. Select a new wallpaper by going to Settings > Wallpaper > Stills.

11. Reset Configurations:
- If problems persist, you can reset all settings without erasing any information. Navigate to General > Reset > Reset All Settings under Settings. Be aware that this will reset your wallpaper and Wi-Fi passwords, among other preferences.

12. Select "Optimize iPhone Storage" from the Settings > Photos > Optimize iPhone Storage menu to enable it. This conserves capacity by storing larger-resolution images and videos in iCloud and retaining smaller copies on your device.

13. Disable Extraneous Effects:
- Disable auto-play message effects and parallax motion effects. Disable "Auto-Play Message Effects" and "Auto-Play Video Previews" under Settings > Accessibility > Motion.

14. Review Location Services:

- Go to Settings > Privacy > Location Services to control which apps can access your location. Turn off location access for any applications that don't need it.

15. Use Low Power Mode:

- When your battery is low, turn on Low Power Mode in Settings. To save power, this briefly disables visual effects and background processes.

You can make sure that your iPhone keeps its best possible performance and responsiveness throughout time by putting these optimization ideas into practice. Adapt these parameters to your usage habits and personal preferences.

4:1 Battery Life Tips

Getting the most out of your iPhone—whether it's the iPhone 15, iPhone Pro, or 15 Pro Max—requires maintaining and maximizing battery life. The following advice can help you maintain and increase the battery life of your iPhone:

1. Upgrade iOS:
 - Update the OS system on your iPhone. Battery performance can be improved by the optimizations and enhancements included in software updates.

 2. Manage Screen Brightness:
 - Go to Settings > Display & Brightness to manually adjust the screen's brightness or to activate Auto-Brightness. Longer battery life can be achieved by reducing brightness.

 3. Activate Low Power Mode:

- When your battery is low, turn on Low Power Mode in Settings. To save power, this mode minimizes visual effects and background activity.

4. Check Battery consumption:
- Go to Settings > Battery to keep an eye on your battery's consumption. Determine which apps use a lot of power and think about changing their settings or setting use limits.

5. Background App Refresh:
- Turn off background app refresh for applications that don't require continual updates. To adjust the settings according to your preferences, go to Settings > General > Background App Refresh.

6. Control Location Services:
- Restrict location access for non-essential apps. To change the location settings for a specific app, navigate to Settings > Privacy > Location Services.

7. Disable Push Email:

- Instead of using Push, configure email accounts to retrieve data manually or more frequently. Navigate to Accounts > Settings > Mail > Fetch New Data.

8. Fetch New Data:
- Reduce the frequency of data fetching if you utilize Push for email. To modify the frequency of fetching, navigate to Settings > Mail > Accounts > Fetch New Data.

9. Use Wi-Fi When Available:
- When Wi-Fi networks are available, connect to them. The power usage of Wi-Fi is lower than that of cellular data.

10. Switch Off Dynamic Wallpapers:
- Motion effects and dynamic wallpapers may use more energy. Under Settings > Wallpaper > Select a New Wallpaper > Stills, select static wallpapers.

11. Examine Background App Refresh:

- Disable this option for any apps that don't need to be updated continuously in the background by going to Settings > General > Background App Refresh.

12. Close Unused Apps:
- Close background-running apps by hand. To remove superfluous apps, double-click the Home button (or, if your smartphone has a Home button, swipe up from the bottom).

13. Optimize Battery Charging:
- Go to Settings > Battery > Battery Health and turn on Optimized Battery Charging. This function shortens the amount of time your iPhone is fully charged, which helps delay battery aging.

14. Switch Off Dynamic Animations:
- Disable effects and animations that are dynamic. Go to Settings > Accessibility > Motion and activate "Reduce Motion."

15. Reset Configurations:

- You don't have to lose any data if you reset all settings if your battery problems persist. Navigate to General > Reset > Reset All Settings under Settings.

By putting these recommendations into practice, you can extend the life of your iPhone's battery and make sure it works at its best all day. Adapt these options to your tastes and usage habits.

4:2 Storage Management

To keep your iPhone running at peak efficiency and to make sure you have enough room for apps, pictures, videos, and other data, effective storage management is essential. The following advice will help you handle storage efficiently:

1. Verify Storage Utilization:
 - To view a detailed breakdown of your storage usage, navigate to Settings > General > [Device] Storage. This displays the apps and data types that are using up the most storage.

2. Delete Unnecessary Apps:
 - Get rid of any apps you aren't using anymore. You can either go to Settings > General > [Device] Storage > tap on the app and choose "Delete App," or you can press and hold an app icon on the Home Screen and tap "Delete App."

3. Clear Safari Cache:

- To free up space taken up by browser cache, scroll down under Settings > Safari and select "Clear History and Website Data".

4. Examine and Remove Images and Videos:

- Remove outdated or superfluous images and videos. To store high-resolution images and videos in iCloud, think about utilizing the "Optimize iPhone Storage" option found under Settings > Photos.

5. Control Podcasts and Music Downloaded:

- Remove any podcasts or music that you no longer require. Additionally, you can use the "Optimize Storage" option under Settings > Music to have downloaded music that you haven't listened to in a long time automatically removed.

6. Delete Downloaded Maps:

- If you use offline maps, select the areas you no longer require by going to Settings > Maps > Downloaded Maps.

7. Verify and Delete Previous Messages:

- Examine and remove previous messages, particularly those that include sizable media attachments. You can modify the message history and automatically delete older messages under Settings > Messages.

8. Use iCloud for Files and Photos:

- Go to Settings > [your name] > iCloud > Photos and turn on iCloud Photos. Additionally, think about storing files on iCloud Drive.

9. Manage App Storage:

- You can enable the "Enable Offload Unused Apps" option to have apps that you don't use frequently automatically removed, or you can offload unused apps in Settings > General > [Device] Storage.

10. Delete Unused Downloads:

- Remove attached files and downloaded files from applications. Look for unused downloads from programs like Files, Dropbox, or other file management apps.

11. Optimize Messages Storage:

- Under Settings > Messages, turn on "Keep Messages" for a set amount of time, and then manually remove older exchanges.

12. Delete Items from Offline Reading Lists:

- If you use Safari's Reading List, remove any items that you have previously read or are no longer in need of offline reading.

13. Examine and Eliminate Podcasts:

- If you download podcasts, make sure to periodically examine and eliminate any episodes that you've finished or no longer require.

14. Delete Unused Documents and Data:

- Look over the "Other" section in Settings > General > [Device] Storage and remove any documents and data from apps that aren't needed.

15. Verify and Control Your iCloud Backup:

- Navigate to Manage Storage > Backups under Settings > [your name] > iCloud. Examine and eliminate outdated backups, or turn off backups for any apps you don't require.

You can improve overall performance on your iPhone by making sure it has enough space for necessary data and apps by putting these storage management tips into practice. Check and tweak these settings frequently according to your storage requirements and usage habits.

4.3 Speed and Efficiency Tricks

Boosting the speed and efficiency of your iPhone involves a combination of tweaking settings, simplifying usage, and managing resources properly. Here are some tips to boost the speed and efficiency of your iPhone:

1. Update iOS:
 - Keep your iOS version up to date. Updates generally contain performance enhancements and bug fixes.

 2. Restart Your iPhone:
 - Regularly restart your device to clear temporary files and refresh system processes, which can assist in improving overall speed.

 3. Reduce Motion and Transparency:
- In Settings > Accessibility > Motion, turn on "Reduce Motion" to decrease animations. Also, in Settings > Accessibility > Display & Text Size, lower transparency.

4. Limit Background App Refresh:

- In Settings > General > Background App Refresh, disable it for programs that don't require real-time updates.

5. Manage Widgets:

- Trash any widgets that aren't needed in the Today View. To access the Today View, swipe right on your Home Screen. To edit widgets, scroll down and hit "Edit".

6. Optimize Location Services:

- Limit location access for apps that don't require it. To change an app's location settings, navigate to Settings > Privacy > Location Services.

7. Check App Updates:

- Keep your apps updated. Developers make updates to improve performance and resolve bugs.

8. Disable Background App Refresh:

- In Settings > General > Background App Refresh, disable this option for apps that don't need regular updates in the background.

9. Reset Settings:
 - If you're encountering persistent troubles, you can reset all settings without deleting data. Select all settings by going to Settings > General > Reset.

10. Clear Safari Cache:
 - In Settings > Safari, scroll down and hit "Clear History and Website Data" to free up space consumed by the browser cache.

11. Optimize Battery Charging:
 - Enable Optimized Battery Charging in Settings > Battery > Battery Health. By shortening the amount of time your iPhone is fully charged, this feature helps delay the aging of your battery.

 12. Use Wi-Fi When Available:

- Connect to Wi-Fi networks when available. Cellular data usage is more energy-intensive than using Wi-Fi.

13. Limited App Notifications:
- Turn off notifications for non-essential applications. Customize each app's notification settings under Settings > Notifications.

14. Review and Delete Old communications:
- Go through and get rid of old communications regularly, particularly the ones that have big media attachments.

15. Manage App Permissions:
- Go to Settings > Privacy and check the permissions of the app for your location, camera, microphone, and other private information. Turn off unused permissions.

16. Optimize Siri:
- In Settings > Siri & Search, adjust Siri's preferences and turn off extra features to improve Siri's efficiency.

17. App Usage Review:

- To find out which apps you use most, check out your Screen Time data in Settings. App usage for non-essentials should be limited.

18. Delete Unused Apps:

- Delete any apps that you have stopped using. To delete an app, either press and hold its icon on the Home Screen and choose "Delete App," or navigate to Settings > General > [Device] Storage > Tap the app and choose "Delete App."

You can enhance the speed and functionality of your iPhone and guarantee a more responsive and seamless user experience by putting these tips into practice. Adapt these configurations to your tastes and usage habits.

CHAPTER 5: ADVANCED CAMERA TECHNIQUES

Whether you have an iPhone 15, Pro, or 15 Pro Max, you can maximize its excellent photo capabilities by using advanced camera techniques. Here are some sophisticated pointers to improve your abilities in photography and videography:

1. Manual Exposure and Focus:
- Press and hold the region of the screen that you wish to adjust for exposure and focus. To manually change exposure, swipe up or down when the yellow box displays.

2. Lock Focus and Exposure:
- Press and hold the screen to activate the AE/AF Lock notification after adjusting focus and exposure. This

makes sure that even if you move the camera, the focus and exposure stay the same.

3. Use Grid Lines:
 - Go to Settings > Camera and turn on the grid lines. This assists you in utilizing the rule of thirds while composing pictures to create more visually appealing images.

4. Shoot in RAW:
 - To take RAW photos, open the Camera app, navigate to Settings > Camera > Formats, and turn on "Apple ProRAW". This gives you more options for editing in the future.

5. Night Mode Photography:
 - Use the Night mode when there is little light. When necessary, it turns on automatically, but you may also manually adjust the exposure duration by tapping the Night mode icon.

 6. Long Exposure Photography:

- Produce effects of long exposure for subjects that are in motion. When using a tripod or a steady surface in Night Mode, the iPhone will automatically prolong the exposure duration.

7. Portrait Mode:
- Try out Portrait mode to get images that appear professional. After shooting the picture, you can alter the aperture, depth, and lighting effects.

8. Pro Video Mode:
- You may capture videos in Pro Video mode in the Camera app, giving you more control over your footage by modifying settings like ISO, shutter speed, and white balance.

9. QuickTake Video:
- To quickly record QuickTake videos, press down the shutter button while in Photo mode. You can continue recording without holding down the button by swiping right to lock the recording.

10. Manual White Balance:

- By tapping the temperature indicator and modifying it based on the lighting, you can manually set the white balance in Pro Video mode.

11. Smart HDR:

- To improve dynamic range, enable Smart HDR. It facilitates the acquisition of additional shadow and highlight detail.

12. Adjust Exposure in Videos:

- Tap the screen to change the exposure while a video is being recorded. The exposure can be locked or allowed to change dynamically.

13. Live Photos:

- Press and hold a photo to explore the movement and sound that was captured in the frame. Additionally, effects like bounce and loop are available.

14. Panorama Shots:

- Select Pano by swiping left in the Camera app to take panoramic pictures. To take a wide-angle picture, go by the instructions displayed on the screen.

15. Ultra-wide and telephoto lenses:
- Make use of the three lenses that your iPhone has to offer: telephoto, wide, and ultra-wide. Play around with different compositions and viewpoints.

16. External Lens Attachments:
- For further imaginative possibilities, think about utilizing external lens attachments. Wide-angle, macro, and fisheye viewpoints are all possible with these lenses.

17. Use the Self-Timer:
- Use the Camera app's self-timer to get steady shots. This lessens the possibility of camera shake when shooting pictures.

18. Third-Party Camera Apps:

- Look into third-party camera apps that provide manual controls, cutting-edge capabilities, and distinctive shooting modes.

Try out these sophisticated camera tricks to improve your iPhone's photography and filmmaking abilities. Explore the functionality of third-party apps and the camera app without hesitation to find new creative opportunities.

5:1 Using the Enhanced Camera System

The impressive camera system of the iPhone 15, iPhone Pro, and iPhone 15 Pro Max enables users to take beautiful pictures and films in a variety of lighting settings. These smartphones take mobile photography to new heights with their strong processing, unique features, and improved sensors.

Main Camera: 48 Megapixels:

The innovative 48 MP primary camera sensor on the iPhone 15 Pro Max produces remarkably clear and detailed photos. Sharper images, less noise, and better low-light performance are made possible by its ultra-high-resolution sensor's ability to capture more light and information.

Sensor-Shift OIS Advancement:

Sensor-shift optical image stabilization, or OIS, is a feature added to the primary camera in the iPhone 15 Pro Max and iPhone Pro. Instead of using lens modifications to compensate for camera shake, sensor-shift OIS moves the sensor itself. With the enhanced stabilization offered by this cutting-edge OIS technology, videos and photos will be smoother and crisper.

Improved Ultra-Wide Lens:

With a bigger sensor and better aperture, the ultra-wide camera on all three models has been upgraded to capture a broader field of view with better resolution and low-light performance. This enables users to accurately record large-scale landscapes, stunning cityscapes, and complex indoor situations.

Upgraded Lens Telephoto Camera:

With an extended focal length and improved telephoto lens, the iPhone 15 Pro Max offers up to 5x optical magnification. With its improved zoom power, users can record far-off subjects in striking detail, which makes it perfect for sports, wildlife photography, and close-ups from a distance.

Movie Mode:

The cinematic mode, which is compatible with all three versions, simulates professional filmmaking skills by adding a depth-of-field effect to films. Videos gain depth and drama with this feature, which automatically focuses on the main subject while blurring the backdrop.

Photonic Motor:

Using computational photography techniques, the Photonic Engine—powered by Apple's A17 Bionic chip—improves image quality under a range of lighting scenarios. It produces amazing images and movies, especially in low light, by using machine learning algorithms to improve exposure, white balance, noise reduction, and detail enhancement.

Evening Mode:

With the much-improved night mode, you can now take even brighter, more detailed photos in low light. All three models' ultra-wide cameras can now take beautiful night photos from a wider angle thanks to the addition of night mode.

Intense Fusion:

All three models come with Deep Fusion, which uses machine learning to improve texture and detail, especially in medium-to-low light. It produces clearer and more defined images by analyzing several exposures of the same image to find and preserve even the smallest details.

Smart HDR 5:

By carefully adjusting exposure and contrast across various areas of an image, Smart HDR 5 outperforms its predecessor and ensures that highlights, shadows, and midtones are captured with the best possible detail. Images as a result appear more balanced and realistic, particularly in scenes with strong contrast.

The iPhone 15, iPhone Pro, and iPhone 15 Pro Max redefine mobile photography with their ground-breaking 48 MP primary camera, sensor-shift OIS, upgraded telephoto and ultra-wide cameras, Cinematic mode, Photonic Engine, improved Night mode, Deep Fusion, and Smart HDR 5. These smartphones raise the bar for mobile imaging by enabling users to take breathtaking images and movies with remarkable clarity, detail, and cinematic quality.

5.2 Photography and Video Tips

Using your iPhone to take beautiful pictures and movies requires a blend of technical expertise and artistic vision. To help you get the most out of your iPhone camera, consider the following photography and video advice:

Advice for Photographers:

1. Apply the Rule of Thirds:
 - To produce a harmonious composition, activate grid lines in your camera settings and arrange important components along the lines or at their intersections.

2. Try Different Views:
 - Take pictures of your subject from various viewpoints and distances to identify the most interesting and distinctive ones.

3. Use Portrait Mode:

- For images with a blurred background that look professional, use Portrait mode. Modify the lighting effects to improve the overall appearance.

4. Make Use of Natural Light:
- Natural light frequently yields the best outcomes. The "golden hours" are sunrise and sunset, when the light is warm and mellow.

5. Tap to Focus:
- Press and hold the region of the screen you wish to concentrate on. This guarantees that your topic is precise and well-defined.

6. HDR for Dynamic Range:
- Turn on HDR (High Dynamic Range) to capture more information in the highlights and shadows, particularly in difficult lighting situations.

7. Use Burst Mode for Action Shots:

- To activate Burst mode, hold down the shutter button. This works well for getting the ideal shot or recording quick motion.

8. Maintain Your Lens Clean:
- To guarantee crisp, clear photos, wipe your camera lens frequently. Having a clean lens is crucial for quality photographs.

9. Explore Live Photos:
- Use Live Photos to capture more than just a still picture. To hear and see the movement and sound that surround a photo, press and hold the image.

10. Try Different Filters:
- Use the Photos app's built-in filters or try out other photo-editing programs to add more flair and emotion to your images.

Video Advice

1. Stabilize Your Shots:

- Hold your iPhone with both hands or use a tripod for smoother videos. Gimbals and other devices are also useful for professional-grade stability.

2. Shoot in Landscape Orientation:
 - For a more visually appealing and cinematic outcome, always shoot videos in landscape orientation.

3. Frame Your Shots:
 - When filming videos, take composition and framing into account. Use captivating viewpoints and don't lose sight of the core topic.

4. Manual Focus and Exposure:
 - To gain more control over your footage, manually change focus and exposure in Pro Video mode.

5. Use Time-Lapse and Slow Motion:
 - Experiment with the Time-Lapse and Slow-Mo modes to create artistic video effects. Time-lapse photography may record long-term changes, while slow motion is excellent for emphasizing details.

6. Test Zoom:

 - Don't overuse the zoom capability, especially on iPhones with multiple lenses that offer optical zoom. Image quality can be lowered via digital zoom.

7. Record Ambient Sound:

 - Be mindful of the audio when filming videos. To give your footage more depth and ambiance, record background noises.

8. Edit Videos on Your iPhone:

 - You may edit and improve your videos straight on your iPhone by using the included iMovie program or third-party video editing apps.

9. Use the Grid:

 - To assist you in creating better video shots, activate the grid lines. For a balanced framing, place important items along the lines or intersections.

10. Capture B-Roll Footage:

- To add interest and diversity to your film, add B-roll, or extra shots, to your main footage.

These techniques can help you improve your iPhone photography and videography, whether you're taking pictures or making films. To let your creativity run wild, don't be scared to try new things and investigate novel approaches.

5:3 Editing and Sharing Media

Thanks to the strong tools and capabilities on your iPhone 15, iPhone Pro, or 15 Pro Max, editing and sharing media is a fluid and creative experience. This section examines your options for editing and sharing content, whether you're developing compelling content or perfecting images or videos.

Photo Editing:

1. Photos App:
 - A variety of editing options are available in the integrated Photos app. To explore options like cropping, altering exposure, color correction, and filter application, open a photo, touch "Edit," and proceed.

2. Markup:
 - Directly add text, drawings, or annotations to your images by using the Markup tool. To access it, select "Edit," then the three-dot icon, and finally "Markup."

3. Portrait Mode Adjustments:

 - After taking the picture, adjust the depth effect for Portrait Mode images. Change the degree of background blur by opening the image in Edit mode.

4. Editing Live Photos:

- Modify Live Photos by selecting a new keyframe, adding effects, or modifying the speed at which they playback. You may make these adjustments directly in the Photos app.

Video Editing:

1. iMovie:

 - More advanced video editing is possible with iMovie, which is accessible on the App Store. Use your iPhone to add effects, music, and transitions to make visually appealing videos.

2. Clips:

- Clips is an easy-to-use app that lets you make entertaining and expressive films. It has functions including animated sticker support, live titles, and filters.

3. Cut, Trim, and Split:
- You may edit movies in the Photos app by dividing clips, chopping pieces, or adjusting the length. With your iPhone, these simple tools let you edit your films more effectively.

Distributing Media:

1. AirDrop:
- Easily share images and movies with AirDrop. To send content wirelessly, open the media file, hit the share icon, choose the recipient's device, and then send it.

2. Messages and Mail:
- Use the Messages or Mail app to send media directly. Type a note or email, hit the camera button, and choose the files you wish to send.

3. Social networking Apps:

- For easy sharing, incorporate your preferred social networking apps, such as Facebook, Instagram, and Twitter. You can edit and share your photographs and videos straight from the apps.

4. iCloud Photo Sharing:

- Use the Photos app to create shared albums and ask loved ones to add photos. All users have access to the shared album and can upload new images or videos.

5. Third-Party Apps:

- For more sophisticated photo editing, check out third-party apps like Adobe Lightroom, Snapseed, or VSCO. Additional filters, effects, and manual tweaks are available in these programs.

6. YouTube and TikTok:

- Post video content straight to YouTube or TikTok. Utilize third-party programs or native editing tools to edit your videos for these platforms.

7. AirPlay:

 - Share your media on a bigger screen by using AirPlay. To share your images or movies with a larger audience, connect to an Apple TV or other device that supports AirPlay.

8. App Automation Shortcuts:

 - Investigate automation with the Shortcuts app. To expedite repetitive actions, such as distributing particular media formats to preset contacts or platforms, create custom shortcuts.

When sharing media, don't forget to review the permissions and privacy settings for each app. With your iPhone 15 series smartphone, you can share your moments and express your creativity with ease thanks to the easy integration of editing tools and a wide range of sharing possibilities.

CHAPTER 6: CONNECTIVITY AND ICLOUD

The iPhone ecosystem is not complete without connectivity and iCloud, which enable smooth data synchronization, storage, and communication between Apple devices. An outline of iCloud and connectivity functions is shown below:

Interconnectivity

1. Cellular and Wi-Fi:
- iPhones are capable of supporting both Wi-Fi and cellular data connectivity. Make sure your smartphone is linked to a dependable Wi-Fi network to experience quicker download speeds and less usage of cellular data.

2. Bluetooth:
- Connect wirelessly to speakers, headphones, and other accessories with Bluetooth. Furthermore, Bluetooth makes it possible for Apple devices to share files via services like AirDrop.

3. AirDrop:

- With AirDrop, you can wirelessly exchange files, movies, documents, and more with other Apple devices that are nearby. Make sure both devices have AirDrop enabled and that Bluetooth and Wi-Fi are turned on.

4. Private WiFi Hotspot:

- To allow other devices to share your iPhone's cellular data connection, turn it into a personal hotspot. When you require internet access for gadgets like a laptop or tablet, this is helpful.

5. Ethernet (via adaptor):

- For a more dependable internet connection, you can connect to a wired Ethernet network on some iPhone models by using a Lightning to Ethernet adaptor.

6. 5G (if supported):

- You can get better internet rates in 5G-covered locations if your iPhone is capable of supporting 5G connectivity.

7. Virtual Private Network (VPN):

- Set up a VPN to protect your internet connection and gain access to content that is geo-blocked.

8. Wi-Fi Calling:
- Use Wi-Fi to make calls when cellular reception is spotty. This function can come in very handy when visiting other countries.

9. Carrier Services:
- Make use of carrier-specific features that improve communication in general, like visual voicemail.

iCloud:

1. iCloud Storage:
- Documents, videos, images, and app data may all be stored in the cloud with iCloud. If necessary, you should upgrade your iCloud storage plan to make sure you have adequate room for data and backups.

2. Automatic Backups:
- Turn on iCloud Backup to periodically backup the data on your iPhone, including settings, applications, and images.

This guarantees that in the event of a loss or upgrade, you can recover your device.

3. Find My iPhone:

- To find a lost or stolen iPhone, use iCloud's Find My iPhone tool. To safeguard your data, you can also remotely delete your device.

4. iCloud Drive:

- Cloud storage is made possible with iCloud Drive, which you can access from any Apple device. It works well with programs like Keynote, Pages, and Numbers.

5. iCloud Photos:

- Save your images and movies in iCloud Photos so you can see them from any Apple device with ease. Additionally, this helps your iPhone's local storage be saved.

6. iCloud Keychain:

- Your passwords and credit card details are safely stored in iCloud Keychain and are available on all of your Apple devices.

7. Family Sharing:

- Configure Family Sharing so that your family can access your iCloud storage, App Store purchases, and Apple Music subscriptions.

8. Mail, Contacts, and Calendars:
- Stay up to date with your contacts, calendars, and emails by having iCloud synchronize data across all your Apple devices.

9. Notes and Reminders:
- You can view and edit your Notes and Reminders from any device thanks to iCloud syncing.

10. Messages in iCloud:
- Turn on Messages in iCloud to sync your iMessages and maintain an up-to-date message history across all of your Apple devices.

A smooth and integrated experience across Apple devices is made possible by both connectivity and iCloud services. They guarantee that your iPhone remains linked to the larger Apple ecosystem and improve data accessibility, security, and collaboration.

6:1 Wi-Fi and Cellular Settings

Setting up your iPhone's Wi-Fi and Cellular settings is essential for dependable internet access and efficient data use control. This is a manual for utilizing and maximizing these settings:

Configuring Wi-Fi

1. Join a Wireless Network:
 - Toggle the switch to activate Wi-Fi by going to Settings > Wi-Fi. From the list of available networks, pick one and, if necessary, enter the password.

2. Ignore the Wi-Fi Network:
 - To eliminate a Wi-Fi network that you have stored, navigate to Settings > Wi-Fi, tap the information button adjacent to the network, and choose "Forget This Network."

 3. Wi-Fi Network Auto-Join:

- You can activate or deactivate the "Auto-Join" function in the Wi-Fi settings. This establishes if your iPhone connects to recognized Wi-Fi networks automatically.

4. Wi-Fi Assist:
- In situations where Wi-Fi connectivity is inadequate, Wi-Fi Assist enables your iPhone to use cellular data. This option is located under Settings > Cellular > Wi-Fi Assistance.

5. Private Wi-Fi Addresses:
- Turn on the "Private Address" setting in Wi-Fi settings to improve privacy. This increases the difficulty for advertising to follow your device using its Wi-Fi MAC address.

6. Networking over WiFi:
- You can stop your device from using Bluetooth and Wi-Fi networks for location accuracy by disabling "Wi-Fi Networking" under Settings > Privacy > Location Services > System Services.

Configuring Cellular Settings:

1. Activate Cellular Data:
- To activate cellular data, navigate to Settings > Cellular and flip the switch next to "Cellular Data."

2. Control Cellular Data Utilization: Data use for individual apps may be viewed under Cellular Settings. To properly manage your cellular data, set data restrictions, turn on Low Data Mode, and turn off data for particular applications.

3. Personal Hotspot:
- Create a personal hotspot to allow you to share your mobile data connection with other devices. The hotspot settings can be adjusted by going to Settings > Cellular > Personal Hotspot.

4. Roaming:
- Go to Settings > Cellular > Cellular Data Options > Data Roaming to allow or disable data roaming while you're not in your native country.

5. Mobile Information Network:

- Advanced users can go to Settings > Cellular > Cellular Data Options > Cellular Data Network to view the Cellular Data Network settings. You may set up APN settings for specific carriers here.

6. Wi-Fi Calling:

- Go to Settings > Phone > Wi-Fi Calling and turn on Wi-Fi calling. This lets you use Wi-Fi to make calls in situations where cellular reception is spotty.

7. Carrier Services:

- Go to Settings > Cellular to see if any carrier-specific services are available. Visual voicemail is one of the extra options that certain carriers provide.

8. Cellular Plan:

- Go to Settings > Cellular > Cellular Data Plan to manage your cellular plan, view usage, and explore more options.

9. Cellular Statistics Reset:

- Navigate to Settings > Cellular and select the "Reset Statistics" option at the bottom to reset data consumption information.

10. Cellular Updates:

- Go to Settings > General > About to periodically check for carrier updates. Updates from carriers may include fixes for bugs and enhancements to cellular connectivity.

You may successfully manage your data on your iPhone and keep a dependable internet connection by adjusting these Wi-Fi and Cellular settings based on your preferences and usage habits.

6.2 iCloud Services and Backup

Apple offers a set of cloud-based services called iCloud, which work in unison with your iPhone and other Apple devices. One of its main features is iCloud Backup, which provides a convenient and safe way to protect the data on your iPhone. An outline of iCloud services and the significance of iCloud backup is provided below:

Services on iCloud:

1. iCloud Drive:
- With iCloud Drive, you can save files, documents, and images in the cloud and have them accessible from any Apple device.

2. iCloud Photos:

- Use iCloud Photos to save your whole collection of images and videos. All devices automatically synchronize changes made on one.

3. Find My:
- Locate your Apple devices with the Find My app, share your whereabouts with loved ones, and remotely wipe your device in the event that it is lost or stolen.

4. iCloud Keychain:
- Stores your credit card details, Wi-Fi passwords, and passwords securely on all of your Apple devices.

5. Mail, Contacts, and Calendars:
- All of your Apple devices are synced with each other's calendars, contacts, emails, and reminders thanks to iCloud.

6. Notes and Reminders:
- Use iCloud syncing to keep your notes and reminders current across devices.

7. Pages, Numbers, and Keynote:

- Using Pages, Numbers, and Keynote, iCloud allows for real-time collaborative work on documents, spreadsheets, and presentations.

8. iCloud Backup:

- Make sure you can restore your iPhone in case something goes wrong by automatically backing up your device's settings, app data, messages, and more to iCloud.

9. Family Sharing:

- Give family members access to apps, music, and other items you've bought. Family members can add to calendars and photo albums that are shared.

10. iCloud Storage Plans:

- Buy more iCloud storage beyond the 5 GB of free space. Plans that accommodate a range of storage needs are available from 50 GB to 2 TB.

iCloud Data Backup:

1. Activate iCloud Backup:

 - Toggle the switch under Settings > [your name] > iCloud > iCloud Backup to activate iCloud Backup.

2. Automated Backups:

- When your device is plugged in, locked, and connected to Wi-Fi, iCloud Backup backs it up automatically. Another option is to manually start a backup.

3. What's in the Backup:

- App data, device settings, iMessages, pictures, and more are all included in iCloud Backup. Media that has previously been bought from Apple Music, the App Store, or iTunes is not included.

4. Manage Backup Storage:

 - Go to Settings > [your name] > iCloud > Manage Storage to view and control your iCloud storage. You can view what's occupying space here and buy extra storage if necessary.

5. Restore from iCloud Backup:

- To transfer your data when configuring a new device or restoring an old one, pick "Restore from iCloud Backup" and specify which backup you want to use.

6. What's Not Included in Backup:

- For security reasons, some data, such as Apple Pay credentials and Face ID preferences, are not included in iCloud Backup. These require manual setup.

7. Delete Backups:

- Go to Settings > [your name] > iCloud > Manage Storage > Backups to manage and remove any existing backups. If you wish to free up iCloud storage, this may be helpful.

8. iCloud Backup with Apple One:

- Additional services like Apple Music, Apple TV +, Apple Arcade, and more are included in Apple One subscription bundles, which also include a variety of iCloud storage options.

For a flawless and safe Apple device experience, make sure that iCloud services are set up and frequently backed up. Specifically, iCloud Backup offers a data safety net by enabling you to restore your device in the event of loss, damage, or an upgrade to a new one.

6:3 AirDrop and Continuity Features

Two strong components of the Apple ecosystem, AirDrop, and Continuity, are intended to improve smooth connectivity and cooperation between Apple devices.

AirDrop:

1. What is AirDrop?
 - AirDrop enables wireless sharing of documents, videos, images, and other content between Apple devices that are near each other.

2. AirDrop Usage Instructions:
   - Turn on both Wi-Fi and Bluetooth devices.
   - Open Control Center on your iPhone, and select "Everyone" or "Contacts Only" from the AirDrop menu.
   - After selecting the desired recipient from the AirDrop list, hit the share icon to share the selected content.

3. Compatibility:

- Devices that support AirDrop include Macs, iPads, iPod Touches, and iPhones.

4. Security:

- End-to-end encryption is used by AirDrop to ensure secure file transfers. To facilitate the transfer, devices must be physically close to one another.

5. AirDrop Settings:

- Navigate to Settings > General > AirDrop to access AirDrop settings. You have the option of allowing content to be sent to you by contacts only, everyone, or receiving off.

Features of Continuity:

1. Handoff:

- you may move between Apple devices with ease. Take an email, for instance, and begin it on your iPhone, then finish it on your Mac.

2. Universal Clipboard:

- Use Universal Clipboard to copy and paste text, photos, or movies from one Apple device to another.

3. Mac Phone Calls:

- Use the cellular connection on your iPhone to make and receive phone calls on your Mac. Both devices must be connected to the same Wi-Fi network and have active iCloud accounts.

4. iMessage and SMS on Mac:

- Utilize your Mac to send and receive iMessages and SMSs. Conversations can be carried on with ease since messages are synchronized across devices.

5. Instant Hotspot:

- Without entering a password, use your iPhone's cellular connection to create an instant hotspot for your Mac or other Apple devices.

6. Requirements:

- Devices must be linked to the same Wi-Fi network and logged into the same iCloud account to use continuity capabilities.

7. Handoff Setup:
 - Toggle "Handoff" on by going to Settings on your iPhone, selecting General > AirPlay & Handoff.

8. Universal Clipboard Setup:
- Make sure that both devices have Bluetooth and Wi-Fi turned on, and that Handoff is enabled.

9. Instant Hotspot Setup:
- Make sure your iPhone is in Settings > Cellular > Personal Hotspot, and that both Wi-Fi and Bluetooth are turned on.

10. Set Up Phone Calls and Messages:
 - To ensure a smooth connection, activate "Text Message Forwarding" and "iPhone Cellular Calls" in the FaceTime settings.

Using a unified ecosystem made possible by AirDrop and Continuity, you can share content and travel between your Apple devices with ease. By removing obstacles, these tools improve productivity and teamwork in your iPhone.

CHAPTER 7: CUSTOMIZING YOUR EXPERIENCE

You may customize your iPhone experience to make it more efficient and unique by adjusting it to your tastes. Here are some ideas for personalizing your iPhone:

1. Customize your home screen:
- App Layout: Long-press an app icon to activate jiggle mode; drag applications to arrange them into folders or create new ones.

- Devices: To facilitate fast access to information, add and personalize widgets to your home screen. To add widgets, swipe left on the Home Screen, then press "Edit".

2. Themes and Wallpaper:

- Select a wallpaper that captures your flair. Select a new wallpaper by going to Settings > Wallpaper. Dynamic wallpapers that alter depending on the time of day are possible with some themes.

3. App Icons and Shortcuts:
- Use Shortcuts to create unique app icons. For a customized appearance, you can select icons, give them unique names, and arrange them on your home screen.

4. Dark Mode:
 - Turn on Dark Mode to see things differently. Click on Appearance > Display & Brightness > Settings, then choose "Dark."

5. Custom Sounds and Ringtones:
 - Customize notification sounds and ringtones for contacts. To alter the sound alerts on your device, navigate to Settings > Sounds & Haptics.

6. Personalized Keyboards:

- Install alternative keyboards to have a unique typing experience. To add and manage keyboards, navigate to Settings > General > Keyboard > Keyboards.

7. Gestures and Accessibility:
- Go to Settings > Accessibility to personalize gestures and accessibility options. AssistiveTouch and touch accommodations are two features that can improve how you interact with the device.

8. Control Center Customization:
- Make the necessary adjustments to the Control Center to include the controls you want. To add, remove, or reorganize controls, navigate to Settings > Control Center > Customize Controls.

9. Siri Shortcuts:
- To automate chores and actions, create Siri Shortcuts. Using the Shortcuts app, you can create personalized voice commands and routines.

10. Privacy Settings:

- Go to Settings > Privacy to review and modify privacy settings. To fit your tastes, control location access, app permissions, and other privacy options.

11. Home App and Smart Home Devices:
- To manage smart home appliances, utilize the Home app. Personalized room configurations, automation, and scenes ensure a flawless smart home experience.

12. App-Specific Settings:
- Go through the settings of each app to personalize your experience with it. Customization options for themes, notifications, and preferences are available in many programs.

13. Perspective Zoom and Dynamic Wallpapers:
- Go to Settings > Wallpaper > Select a New Wallpaper to enable or disable Perspective Zoom for wallpapers. This modifies the parallax effect of the wallpaper as your device tilts.

14. Reading Preferences:

- Adjust Safari's reading preferences. For a customized reading experience, change the font sizes, activate Reader View, or utilize the Reading List.

15. Notifications and Mail:
- To effectively arrange your mailbox, use the Mail settings. To control alerts, go to Settings > Notifications and adjust the notification settings for each app.

16 . Touch ID and Face ID:
- To ensure security and convenience, adjust the Face ID or Touch ID settings. To alter biometric authentication, go to Settings > Face ID & Passcode or Touch ID & Passcode.

17. App Library Organization:
- Sort apps in the App Library according to their respective categories. On your Home Screen, swipe left to open the App Library.

18. iCloud Settings:

- Go to Settings > [your name] > iCloud to customize your iCloud settings. Select which files to sync, turn on iCloud Drive, and control other iCloud functions.

19. Screen Time:
- Configure Screen Time to keep an eye on and manage the use of your devices. Go to Settings > Screen Time to customize app limits, downtime, and content controls.

20. Personalized Fonts:
- You can use custom fonts with some apps. Use the Fonts settings under Settings > Display & Brightness, or check the settings for each specific app.

With these customization choices, you can be confident that your iPhone will meet your needs and preferences, making it a more efficient and pleasurable gadget overall. Examine these options and modify them according to your device's usage.

7:1 Personalizing Your IPhone

Customizing the look of your iPhone is just one aspect of personalizing it; another is making it seem like it's only yours. This guide will assist you in customizing many elements of your iPhone:

1. App Layout:
- Home Screen Aesthetics: Sort your apps by color or by how they are used. Make folders to help your Home Screen look cleaner.
  - Devices: Include widgets that offer information at a glance. To give them a unique touch, adjust their size and positioning.

2. Themes and Wallpapers:
  - Select wall coverings that complement your taste. Use your images or experiment with dynamic wallpapers that alter according to the time of day.
  - Look through the App Store's themes to customize the appearance of your interface and icons.

3. Custom App Icons:

 - To make custom app icons, use the Shortcuts app.
Select pictures and use them as icons for your preferred
apps to customize the look of your Home Screen.

4. Dynamic Widgets: Use dynamic widgets to quickly
get personalized information. You can set them up with
information on health, calendar events, and weather
according to your preferences.

 5. Light or Dark Mode:

 - Change the mode between Light and Dark depending
on the time of day or your preferences. To choose,
navigate to Settings > Display & Brightness.

 6. Sounds and Ringtones:

 - Customize your contacts' notification noises and
ringtones. Select noises that speak to you or make your
own.

 7. Personalized Keyboards:

- Examine keyboards from third parties that have different layouts and themes. Make typing more enjoyable by selecting a keyboard that complements your style.

8. Control Center Shortcuts:
- Add shortcuts to your frequently used features to personalize the Control Center. Go to Settings > Control Center > Customize Controls to add or remove controls.

9. Siri and Voice Feedback:
- Train Siri to recognize your voice to make it more unique. To adjust Siri's voice feedback, navigate to Settings > Siri & Search > My Siri Voice.

10. Widgets for the Home Screen:
- Look into apps from third parties that provide different widgets for your Home Screen. These widgets can offer a personalized touch to everything from calendar events to weather.

11. Home App and Smart Home Devices:

- Configure your smart home devices with the Home app. Customize room names, automation, and scenarios to reflect your tastes.

12. App-Specific Customization:
 - Tailor your experience by going into each app's specific settings. Numerous programs come with customization capabilities, layout options, and themes.

13. Dynamic Wallpapers and Perspective Zoom:
 - To adjust the parallax effect, try out different dynamic wallpapers or turn off Perspective Zoom under Settings > Wallpaper.

 14. Reading Preferences:
- Adjust Safari's reading preferences. For a customized reading experience, change the font sizes, activate Reader View, or utilize the Reading List.

15. Mail and Notifications:

- Customize notification preferences and email signatures to provide a more customized communication experience.

16 . Touch ID and Face ID:
- For convenience, personalize the Face ID or Touch ID settings. Go to Settings > Face ID & Passcode or Touch ID & Passcode to change the authentication settings.

17. App Library Organization:
- Rearrange app categories to personalize the App Library. On your Home Screen, swipe left to open the App Library.

18. iCloud Configuration:
- Go to Settings > [your name] > iCloud to customize your iCloud settings. Select which files to sync, turn on iCloud Drive, and control other iCloud functions.

19. Screen Time Insights:

- Configure Screen Time to gain knowledge about how you use your device. Go to Settings > Screen Time to customize the downtime and limit settings.

20. Personalized Accessories:
- Customize the look of your iPhone with distinctive covers, wallpapers, and accessories.

Customizing your iPhone is a continuous process that changes based on your tastes. Try using these settings to make your iPhone experience feel like it's entirely your own.

7.2 App Management and Organization

A smooth and clutter-free user experience on your iPhone is a result of effective app management and organization. The following advice will help you efficiently manage and arrange your apps:

1. Organization of the Home Screen:
- often Used Apps: Arrange your most often used apps for easy access on the Home Screen.
   - Holders: Sort comparable programs into folders. iOS will automatically create a folder when you drag one app onto another.

2. App Library:
- To access the App Library, swipe left on your home screen. Your apps are automatically categorized, making it simpler to locate and open them without taking up too much space on the Home Screen.

 3. App Dock:

- Arrange your most important apps in the app dock, which is located at the bottom of your Home Screen. You can access it from any page on the Home Screen.

4. Devices:
- You can add widgets to your home screen to display information quickly. Long-press the Home Screen, and select the widgets you want by tapping the '+' symbol.

5. Delete Unnecessary Apps:
 - Get rid of any apps you aren't using anymore. Tap the 'X' icon to remove an app after long-pressing it until it goes into jiggle mode. Pre-installed apps are not deleted; rather, they are moved from the Home Screen.

6. Updates for the App:
 - Update your programs frequently to take advantage of new features, enhancements, and security patches. To guarantee you're always running the most recent versions, enable automatic updates under Settings > App Store.

7. Search Function:

- Swipe down on the Home Screen to access the search function. It's a fast method of finding and opening programs without having to navigate between sites.

8. Reset Layout of Home Screen:

- Navigate to Settings > General > Reset > Reset Home Screen Layout if your Home Screen is jumbled. This restores the layout to its original configuration.

9. App Pages to Hide:

- It is possible to hide entire app pages to minimize clutter. To uncheck the sites you wish to conceal, long-press on a blank area of the Home Screen, tap the three dots at the bottom, and then select them.

10. App Store Categories:

- Look through the App Store's categories to find fresh apps. When you select the 'Apps' option, several categories will appear to assist you in finding apps that are specific to your interests.

11. App Notifications:

- Go to Settings > Notifications to control app alerts. For a less distracted experience, customize which apps can give you notifications and change their settings.

12. Organize by Usage:

- Sort programs according to how they are used. Sort apps by category: put work apps in one folder, play apps in another, and so on.

13. Make Use of App Shortcuts:

- Certain app icons can be revealed by long-pressing them. Some apps use these shortcuts to offer fast operations or to give users access to particular features.

14. App Offloading:

- Go to Settings > General > Offload Unused Apps and turn it on. Storage on [Device]. With this function, apps you don't use often are deleted but their data is retained. The app icon is still there, and you can download it again if necessary.

15. Screen Time restrictions:

- Go into Settings and use Screen Time to set usage restrictions for apps. It aids in screen time management and control for a more healthful digital experience.

16. Intelligent Family:

- You can arrange shared purchases and apps if you have a Family Sharing subscription. Navigate to Settings > [your name] > Family Sharing to access the Family Sharing settings.

17. Configuration for Accessibility:

- Click Settings > Accessibility to view accessibility settings. For a more user-friendly experience, change the parameters to suit certain requirements or preferences.

18. Backup and Restore:

- Use iTunes or iCloud to regularly back up your iPhone. In the unlikely event that you need to restore your smartphone, this guarantees you have a duplicate of your settings, organization, and app data.

19. App-Specific Organization:
- Tailor settings to the specific applications. You can arrange material, make folders, and customize your experience with a lot of apps.

20. Application Managers from Third Parties:
 - Check out the App Store's third-party app management solutions. Certain apps come with sophisticated capabilities that help you manage, sort, and arrange your apps more effectively.

You can keep your iPhone's app ecosystem efficient and well-organized by following these suggestions, which will make it simpler for you to locate and utilize the apps that are most important to you.

7.3 Accessibility Features

To ensure that users with varying requirements and preferences can use their iPhones efficiently and pleasantly, iOS offers a comprehensive set of accessibility features. Below is a summary of some of the most important accessibility features in iOS:

1. VoiceOver:
 - Description: VoiceOver is a screen reader that reads text on the screen aloud, enabling those with vision difficulties to view it.
   - Activation: VoiceOver under Settings > Accessibility.

2. Zoom:
 - Description: Zoom allows users who want a larger display or who have visual impairments to alter the magnification.
   - Activation: Zoom under Settings > Accessibility.

3. Magnifier:

- Description: Convert your iPhone into a magnifying glass to enable real-time item zooming.
   - Activation: Magnifier under Settings > Accessibility.

4. Description & Text Size:
 - Description: Modify contrast, bold text, and text size to improve visibility.
   - Activation: Accessibility > Display & Text Size under Settings.

5. Color Filters:
 - Description: Modify the display colors to suit users with different visual preferences or those who are color blind.
   - Activation: Display & Text Size > Color Filters under Settings > Accessibility.

6. Voice Control:
 - Description: Use voice commands to navigate and operate your device. beneficial for people who have motor impairments.

- Activation: Voice Control under Settings > Accessibility.

7. Siri Shortcuts:
 - Description: Customize voice commands and shortcuts to make difficult jobs easier.
   - Activation: Siri Shortcuts under Settings > Accessibility > Siri.

8. Switch Control:
 - Description: To operate your device, use touch or facial recognition on the iPhone, or connect an external adaptable device.
   - Activation: Switch Control under Settings > Accessibility.

 9. AssistiveTouch:
 - Description: Provide a virtual touch interface that allows people with motor difficulties to interact with taps, swipes, and gestures.
   - Activation: AssistiveTouch under Settings > Accessibility > Touch.

10. Speak Screen:

- Description: Use a simple swipe gesture to have the screen's information read aloud.

  - Activation: Select Speak Screen under Settings > Accessibility > Spoken Content.

11. Captioning & Subtitles:

- Description: Add personalized captions and subtitles to videos to improve accessibility for people with hearing loss.

  - Activation: Accessibility > Settings > Captioning & Subtitles.

12. Sound Recognition:

- Description: Get alerts when significant noises, such as doorbells, sirens, or alarms, occur.

  - Activation: Sound Recognition under Settings > Accessibility.

13. Touch Accommodations:

- Description: Modify touch settings to take into account various motor difficulties or touch sensitivity levels.

   - Activation: Touch Accommodations under Settings > Accessibility > Touch.

14. Dictation:

- Description: Enter text into a variety of apps by using voice-to-text dictation.

   - Activation: Voice Dictation under Settings > Accessibility > Voice Control.

15. Guided Access:

- Description: Control which functions are available and keep your device usage limited to a particular app.

   - Activation: Guided Access under Settings > Accessibility.

16. Accessibility Shortcut:

- Description: Set up a home or side button triple-click to swiftly access specific accessibility features.

   - Activation: Accessibility Shortcut under Settings > Accessibility.

17. rear Tap:

- Description: Tapping the rear of your iPhone allows you to customize actions. beneficial for those who have motor impairments.

  - Activation: Touch > Back Tap under Settings > Accessibility.

18. Braille Display Integration:

- Description: Use your iPhone to connect a Braille display for navigation and tactile feedback.

  - Activation: VoiceOver > Braille under Settings > Accessibility.

19. Speak Screen in Safari:

- Description: Turn on Speak Screen in Safari to hear website information read aloud.

  - Switching On Safari > Open a webpage > Toggle on Speak Screen by swiping down with two fingers.

20. Emergency SOS:

- Description: Press the side button five times to quickly disclose your position and contact emergency personnel.

- Activation: Go to Settings > SOS for emergencies.

CHAPTER 8: TROUBLESHOOTING AND MAINTENANCE

Maintaining and troubleshooting your iPhone is crucial to keeping it operating effectively and taking care of any potential problems. The following general advice can be used to solve typical issues and carry out maintenance tasks:

Fixing Issues:

1. Try Again with Your iPhone:
- Minor problems are often solved with a simple restart. Turn it off, wait a few seconds, and then power on your iPhone again.

2. Inspect for Software Updates:

- Verify that the most recent iOS version is installed on your iPhone. To find and install updates, navigate to Settings > General > Software Update.

3. Clear Storage Space:
- Performance problems may arise if your iPhone's storage is low. You can either use the "Offload Unused Apps" function found in Settings > General > [Device] Storage or remove superfluous apps, pictures, and videos.

4. Close Background Apps:
- To free up system resources, close any background-running apps. To remove apps you're not using, double-click the Home button (or slide up from the bottom on more recent models).

5. Reset Settings:
- You can reset settings without erasing your data if you're having ongoing problems. Navigate to General > Reset > Reset All Settings under Settings.

6. Check Network Connection:

 - If you're experiencing problems connecting, make sure that your network is reliable and that Wi-Fi or cellular data is turned on.

7. Force Restart:

 - Try a force restart if your iPhone stops responding. The process differs according to the model of the iPhone; see Apple's official documentation for details.

8. Clear Safari Cache:

 - Clear the cache in Safari if it's sluggish or unresponsive. Navigate to Settings > Safari > Delete Website Data and History.

9. Reset Network Settings:

 - Go to Settings > General > Reset > Reset Network Settings to reset the network settings if you're having issues with it.

10. Restore from Backup:

- If everything else fails, you can use iTunes or iCloud to restore your iPhone from a backup. Before doing a restoration, make sure you have a backup of your data.

Upkeep:

1. Regular Backups:
- Make sure you routinely use iTunes or iCloud to back up your data. This is important in case you lose your data or need to restore your iPhone.

2. Clean Your iPhone:
- Using a soft, lint-free cloth, gently clean the outside of your iPhone. Steer clear of cleaning supplies and use caution while near buttons and ports.

3. Update Apps:
- You can manually update your apps from the App Store or enable automatic updates to keep them current. Performance enhancements and bug fixes are frequently included in updated programs.

4. Optimize Battery Health:

 - Go to Settings > Battery > Battery Health and periodically assess the condition of your battery. Get a new battery if the condition of your current one has greatly declined.

5. Manage App Permissions:

 - Go to Settings > Privacy to examine and control the permissions for your app. Verify that apps have the required permissions, and if necessary, remote access.

6. Monitor Storage Usage:

 - Go to Settings > General > [Device] Storage to monitor how much space is being used by your device. To make room, delete any programs, pictures, and movies that aren't needed.

7. Adjust Notification Settings:

 - To cut down on pointless alerts and enhance efficiency, personalize notification settings under Settings > Notifications.

8. Examine the Background App Refresh:

- Go to Settings > General > Background App Refresh to adjust the settings. Turn it off for apps that don't need to be updated frequently.

9. Evaluate Location Services:

 - Go to Settings > Privacy > Location Services to review and control app access to location services. Turn off location access for any unnecessary apps.

10. As a Final Option, Factory Reset:

- If all attempts have been exhausted and problems remain, a factory reset may be necessary. Before proceeding, make sure you have a backup of your data. Go to Erase All Content and Settings under Settings > General > Reset.

Your iPhone will run smoothly and effectively if you adhere to these troubleshooting and maintenance advice. You can improve your overall experience with your device by regularly checking for updates and changing its settings.

8:1 Common Issues and Solutions

With iPhones, common problems can occasionally occur, although many of them have simple fixes. The following list of typical iPhone problems and their fixes is provided:

1. Quick Battery Drain:
 - Solution:

   - Go to Settings > Battery > Battery Health to check the condition of the battery. If it's severely damaged, you might want to get a new battery.

   - To save battery life, minimize background app refreshes, turn off unused location services, and reduce screen brightness.

   - End background-running applications.

 2. Problems with Wi-Fi Connections: - Solution:

   - Turn on the Wi-Fi router and your iPhone again.

   - Go to Settings > Wi-Fi, forget the network, and then reconnect.

- Choose Settings > General > Reset > Reset Network Settings to reset the network settings.

3. Problems with Bluetooth Connectivity:
 - Solution:
   - Go to Settings and turn on and off Bluetooth.
   - Go to Settings > Bluetooth, forget the device, and then reconnect.
   - Turn on both the Bluetooth device and your iPhone.

4. App Freezes or Crashes:
 - Solution:
   - Install the most recent version of the software.
   - Turn your iPhone back on.
   - Remove the troublesome app and reinstall it.

5. Inoperable Touchscreen:
 - Solution:
   - Wipe your hands and the screen.
   - Turn your iPhone back on.
   - Force a restart if the issue persists.

6. Inoperative Cellular Data:

 - Solution:

   - Go to Settings and turn on and off cellular data.

   - Turn your iPhone back on.

   Look for updates from your carrier under Settings > General > About.

7. iCloud Sync Problems:

 - Solution:

   - Visit Apple's system status page to check the status of your iCloud.

   - Log out and then back into iCloud.

   Verify that you have enough storage on iCloud.

8. Mobile Overheating:

 - Solution:

   - If the device overheats while being charged, remove the case.

   - End processor-intensive chores and close any background applications.

   - Steer clear of using your iPhone in the sun.

9. Inability to Use Touch ID or Face ID:

- Solution:

Verify that your fingerprint or face has been properly enrolled.

- Wash your hands and the Face ID or Touch ID sensor.

- If problems still arise, reset the Face ID or Touch ID settings.

10. Delayed Performance:

- Solution:

- Shut down any open apps.

- Make storage space available by removing unneeded programs or data.

- Turn your iPhone back on.

11. Incapable of Updating iOS:

- Solution:

Make sure your iPhone has enough battery life and is linked to Wi-Fi.

- Retry after deleting the downloaded update.

If over-the-air upgrades don't work, update using iTunes.

12. Audio Not Working or Distorted:
 - Solution:

Examine the physical mute switch located on your iPhone's side.

- Modify the volume and make sure the Do Not Disturb feature is off.

- Turn your iPhone back on.

13. GPS Not Functioning:
 - Solution:

Go to Settings > Privacy > Location Services to activate location services.

- Turn your iPhone back on.

- Look for available iOS updates and install them.

14. Cannot Make or Receive Calls:
- Solution:

- Verify the strength of your cellular signal.

- Turn your iPhone back on.

- Speak with your carrier to make sure there are no problems with your account.

15. Inability to Send or Receive Texts:
 - Solution:
- Verify your Wi-Fi and cellular signal.
    - Turn your iPhone back on.
    Verify that Settings > Messages does not contain any SMS restrictions.

16. Lack of Storage Nearly Completed: - Solution:
    - Clear the Safari cache and remove any unnecessary apps.
    - Organize and remove outdated pictures and videos.
    - Move files to a PC or use cloud storage.

17. Inexplicable Restarts or Shutdowns: - Solution:
- Upgrade to the most recent iOS version.
    Look for updates for the app.
    If problems continue, get in touch with Apple Help.

18. Incapable of Charging:

- Solution:

- Inspect the wall adapter and Lightning cable for damage.

Apply compressed air to the charging port to clean it.

- Try using a different adaptor and charging cord.

19. Lost or Stolen iPhone:

- Solution:

- You can remotely find, lock, or erase your iPhone by using Find My.

- Notify your carrier and the local authorities of the loss.

20. System or Software Failures:

- Solution:

- Update to the most recent version of iOS.

- Execute a hard restart.

- As a last option, restore your iPhone with iTunes.

It is advised to get in touch with Apple Support or visit an Apple Store for expert assistance if you are experiencing persistent troubles or issues not addressed here. Before undertaking any troubleshooting actions that include restoring or resetting your iPhone, always make a backup of your data.

8:2 Software Updates and Security

Updating software and implementing security patches are essential for keeping an iPhone safe and secure. This is an explanation of their importance and how to deal with them:

Updates for Software:

1. Updates Are Important:
 - Updates to the software regularly offer bug fixes, performance enhancements, and new features. They also fix security flaws, improving your iPhone's overall security and functionality.

2. Automatic Updates:
 - Settings > General > Software Update > Customize Automatic Updates is where you may turn on automatic updates. This guarantees that crucial updates are installed on your iPhone in the background.

3. Checking for Updates Manually:

- To check for and install updates manually, navigate to Settings > General > Software Update. Make sure your gadget is plugged in or has enough battery life while it is updating and linked to Wi-Fi.

4. iOS Version Compatibility:

- Verify that your applications work with the most recent iteration of iOS. Updates are frequently released by developers to optimize their apps for new features and operating system modifications.

5. Security Patches:

- Apple fixes vulnerabilities in software by releasing security patches. Updating your iPhone is essential if you want to keep it safe from possible security risks.

Safety Procedures:

1. Biometrics and Passcodes:

- For device security, set up a strong passcode or utilize Touch ID or Face ID. This shields your iPhone from unwanted access.

2. Two-Factor Authentication (2FA):
- Set up your Apple ID to use Two-Factor Authentication. This enhances security further, particularly for iCloud and other Apple services.

3. App Permissions:
 - Check and adjust app permissions frequently under Settings > Privacy. Limit the apps that don't need them to have access to sensitive data like contacts, photographs, and location.

4. Activate Find My iPhone:
- Navigate to Settings > [your name] > Find My > Find My iPhone to access the feature. This function lets you remotely lock or wipe your device and helps you find it if it's lost or stolen.

5. App Store Settings:

- Go to Settings > App Store and change the App Store settings. Enable "Download New Apps" and "App Updates" to make sure that downloading new apps requires authentication and that your apps are updated automatically.

6. Review Connected Apps:
- Examine the services and apps that are linked to your Apple ID regularly. Eliminate any that you don't trust or utilize anymore. Navigate to Settings > [your name] > Password & Security > Apple ID Apps.

7. Secure Wireless Networks:
- Steer clear of unprotected wireless networks. When utilizing public Wi-Fi, stick to trusted networks and think about adding an extra layer of security by using a Virtual Private Network (VPN).

8. Mail and Messages Security:
- To unlock Mail and Messages, enable Face ID or Touch ID. This guarantees the privacy of the contents of your emails and messages.

9. Avoid Jailbreaking:

 - Steer clear of jailbreaking your iPhone since it puts your security at risk. To make sure that the apps you download pass Apple's security inspections, only download them from the App Store.

10. Regular Data Backups:

 - Use iTunes or iCloud to frequently back up the data on your iPhone. This guarantees that in the event of a major problem, theft, or loss of your device, you can recover your data.

11. Report Suspicious behavior:

 - Notify Apple if you come across any suspicious behavior or phishing efforts. Apple offers channels for reporting any threats and takes security seriously.

12. Security Research:

 - Keep up with the most recent security upgrades and threats. You can make educated judgments about the security of your device by being aware of the security warnings that Apple releases regularly.

You can guarantee a safe and dependable iPhone experience by being watchful, updating your software, and adhering to security best practices. Your device and personal data are kept safer overall thanks to Apple's dedication to frequent upgrades and security precautions.

8:3 Physical Care and Maintenance Tips

To maintain the longevity and functionality of your iPhone, you must take good care of it both digitally and physically. The following are some physical upkeep and care guidelines for your iPhone:

1. Use a Protective cover:
 - Invest in a high-quality cover to shield your iPhone from dings, scratches, and accidentally dropped objects. Cases are available in a variety of materials and designs to fit your tastes.

2. Put a Screen Protector on It:
 - Put a tempered glass or film screen protector on the screen of your iPhone to shield it from dings and scratches. To prevent air bubbles, make sure it is positioned accurately.

 3. Avoid Extreme Temperatures:

- 32 to 95 degrees Fahrenheit (0 to 35 degrees Celsius) is the ideal temperature range for iPhones. Keep your gadget away from extremely cold or hot temperatures as they may have an impact on its performance and battery.

4. Maintain it Clean
- Wipe the screen and outside often with a gentle, lint-free cloth. Steer clear of caustic chemicals and abrasive objects, and exercise caution while near ports and buttons.

5. Avoid Submersion in Water:
- iPhones are not completely watertight. Keep your gadget out of the water and make sure it dries completely if it does get wet by accident. If you think you'll be in the wet, use a case that can withstand dampness.

6. Be Aware of Ports:
- Make sure that ports, such as the speaker grills and Lightning connector, are clear of dust and debris. If necessary, clean them with compressed air or a small, soft brush.

7. Handle with Clean Hands:

- Grease and oils can cause touchscreens to become sensitive. Before using your iPhone, wash your hands to avoid bringing grease and oils onto the screen.

8. Keep Safe While Traveling:

- Make sure your iPhone doesn't come into contact with coins, keys, or anything that could scratch it when carrying it in a backpack or pocket. Think about utilizing a special pocket or pouch.

9. Take Care Not to Drop:

- Even while cases offer protection, you should always treat your iPhone carefully. Keep it away from surfaces with edges or places where it might fall by accident.

10. Control Battery Health:

- Protect your iPhone from being overcharged. After the gadget is fully charged, unplug it and use a reliable charger. Additionally, try not to frequently allow the battery to discharge too low.

11. Inspect for Loose Buttons:

- Regularly inspect physical buttons for any anomalies or looseness. Please get in touch with Apple Support if you run into any problems.

12. Remove Case for Cooling:

- Take into consideration taking off the case for a short while to improve heat dissipation if your iPhone tends to warm up while being used or charged.

13. Store in a Safe Location:

- Keep your iPhone in a secure location while not in use. Avoid putting it in direct sunlight or next to heat sources.

14. Software Updates Frequently:

- Updating the software on your iPhone improves efficiency and fixes potential security flaws, all of which contribute to the general well-being of your device.

15. Emergency Backup:

- Make regular backups of your iPhone to iTunes or iCloud in case of physical damage or loss. Having a copy of your data for recovery is ensured by doing this.

You can guarantee that your iPhone maintains its best possible condition and offers a dependable and pleasurable user experience by implementing these physical care and maintenance guidelines into your daily routine.

CHAPTER 9: EXPERT TIPS AND TRICKS

Here are some professional pointers and ideas to
improve using your iPhone:

1. Efficient App Switching:
- Swipe horizontally along the bottom edge of the screen
to quickly switch between frequently used apps.
Multitasking is made seamless with this motion.

2. Customize Control Centre:
- Navigate to Settings > Control Centre > Customize
Controls to add your touch to the Control Centre.
Shortcuts can be added or removed to provide easy
access to key functions.

3. Hidden Trackpad Feature:
- Use the trackpad function on your iPhone to move the
pointer precisely. To move the cursor on a 3D Touch
device, press and hold the keyboard until it becomes
blank, then drag your finger.

4. Long Exposure Photos:

- Take beautiful long-exposure pictures without the use of outside programs. Place your iPhone on a flat surface, open the Camera app, choose a Live Photo, and swipe up to see the "Long Exposure" effect.

5. Easy Camera Access:

- To rapidly access the camera, swipe left on the lock screen. You may easily capture impromptu moments with this shortcut without having to unlock your cell phone.

6. Make Emoji Stickers:

- Utilize Emoji stickers in communication. To utilize the Emoji sticker pack in chats, launch the Messages app, select the Emoji icon, and create your Emoji. An automatic sticker pack will be generated.

7. Hidden Shutter Button in Volume Keys:

- Turn your headphones' volume keys into a remote shutter for the Camera app. This is useful for snapping pictures of your iPhone without having to touch it.

8. Personalized Vibration Sequences:

- Give some contacts unique vibrating patterns. Navigate to Contacts, pick a contact, click Edit, then select "Vibration." Make a unique design with the help of the on-screen tutorial.

9. Shake to Undo:

- You can rapidly undo activities or type on your iPhone by shaking it. This is especially helpful if you've made an unwanted modification or inadvertently erased text.

10. Hidden Dark Mode Scheduling:

- Setup Time for Dark Mode to Turn On Automatically. Navigate to Settings > Display & Brightness > Options > Dark Appearance. Select Custom Schedule and enter the times you'd like.

11. Hidden Battery Percentage:

- The bonus tip for battery is to activate the battery percentage indicator without making it permanent

12. Indicator:

- To see the exact battery % in the Control Centre, touch and hold the battery indicator until it grows.

Making the most of your iPhone is possible with the help of these professional tips and tricks, which provide features and shortcuts that may not be immediately evident in regular use. Try these methods out to find new ways to go about and make effective use of your smartphone.

9:1 Hidden Features and Shortcuts

Discover all of the hidden functions and shortcuts on your iPhone that can improve productivity and add a little convenience to your experience.

1. Back Tap Quick Links:
   - Double-tap or triple-tap the rear of your iPhone to set up an action. Go to Settings > Accessibility > Touch > Rear Tap. This can involve opening an app, snapping a screenshot, and more.

2. Silence Unknown Callers:
   - Turn on "Silence Unknown Callers" under Settings > Phone to block calls from unknown numbers. Voicemail will be the default response for calls from numbers that are not in your contacts, mail, or messages.

3. In real-time:

- You can interact with text in your images with the Camera app's Live Text feature if you're running iOS 15 or later. You can immediately copy, paste, search for, or translate text from your photos.

4. Organization of App Library:
- On your home screen, swipe left to open the App Library. Your apps are automatically categorized, and you can use the recommendations based on your usage or search for apps.

5. Hide Pages from the Home Screen:
- Long-press the home screen, tap the three dots at the bottom and select the pages you wish to keep hidden. This clears the screen of unnecessary pages and minimizes clutter.

6. Text Selection Magnifier:
- Tap, hold, and drag your finger while the text is selected. Text editing becomes more exact when you touch the cursor and transfer it to the desired location for fine control.

7. Optimized Charging:

- Go to Settings > Battery > Battery Health and turn on "Optimized Battery Charging". To cut down battery aging, this feature learns your daily charging habits.

8. Easily Retrieve Recently Closed Tabs:

- Holding down the "+" button in Safari will display a list of recently closed tabs. This is useful for fast-opening tabs that you may have inadvertently closed.

9. Secret Safari Features:

- To move backward or forward in Safari, swipe left or right on the bottom bar. In addition, you can reload settings without content blockers by tapping and holding the refresh button.

10. Keyboard with One Hand:

- You may make typing on larger iPhones easier by turning on a one-handed keyboard. To change the keyboard orientation to the left or right, press and hold the globe or emoticon icon on the keyboard.

11. Easily Flip Between Bluetooth or Wi-Fi Networks:
- To view a list of accessible networks or devices, tap and hold the Wi-Fi or Bluetooth icon in the Control Centre. This makes switching quickly possible without going into Settings.

12. Search Emojis:
- When you input a word in the text field while using the emoji keyboard, iOS will recommend appropriate emojis. If you're having trouble finding the specific emoji, this comes in helpful.

13. Customize AirPods Controls:
- Go to Settings > Bluetooth > (Your AirPods) > Customize AirPods controls. Either press left or right. Give distinct purposes to the double-tap and press-and-hold motions.

14. Easy Access Camera Timer:

- To select a 3- or 10-second timer, hit the timer icon in the Camera app. This helps organize group portraits or get steady photographs.

15. Caps Lock Shortcut:
- To activate Caps Lock, double-tap the Shift key on the keyboard. You may quickly type all capital letters without holding the key by using this method.

These iPhone shortcuts and secret functions demonstrate the breadth of its capability and improve the efficiency and enjoyment of daily tasks. Try out these choices to see which ones work best for your preferences and workflow.

9.2 Advanced Settings and Customizations

Open the advanced settings and modifications to personalize your iPhone experience. This is a tutorial to help you discover your device's more advanced features:

1. Accessibility Shortcuts:
- Create shortcuts for accessibility features to get to them quickly, such as AssistiveTouch, VoiceOver, and Magnifier. To modify these shortcuts, navigate to Settings > Accessibility > Accessibility Shortcut.

2. Guided Access for Focus:
- To restrict your iPhone to only one app when focusing on a task, like reading or studying, use Guided Access (Settings > Accessibility > Guided Access).

3. Customization of the App Library:
- You can hide or expose particular app categories in the App Library. To customize the App Library, long-press

on the home screen, hit the dots at the bottom, and deselect categories.

4. Widgets for the Home Screen:
 - You can add widgets to your home screen to acquire information at a glance. To alter your layout, long-press the home screen, tap the "+" symbol, and choose widgets.

5. Personalized Vibrations:
 - Make personalized vibrations for your contacts. To create a custom vibration pattern, go to Contacts, choose a contact, touch Edit, and select "Vibration".

6. Personalized Siri Responses:
 - Teach Siri to identify your voice to provide you with customized replies. To teach Siri to recognize your voice, navigate to Settings > Siri & Search > Siri Voice.

7. A Different Face ID Appearance:
 - Train Face ID to identify a different appearance. ideal for identifying your face in a variety of accessories or

haircuts. Establish a Different Appearance under Settings > Face ID & Passcode.

8. secret Album in Photos:
 - Conceal images within a secret album. Pick pictures, press the share symbol, then select "Hide." Go to the Albums tab in the Photos app to view the hidden album.

 9. FaceTime Attention Correction:
 - To create the appearance of eye contact during FaceTime chats, turn on "FaceTime Attention Correction" in Settings > FaceTime.

 10. Mail Swipe Actions:
 - Personalize the Mail app's swipe actions. To set up actions like Mark as Read, Flag, or Archive, navigate to Settings > Mail > Swipe Options.

 11. Custom Mailboxes:
 - In the Mail app, create custom mailboxes. To effectively arrange your emails, long-press the mailbox list, select "New Mailbox," and proceed.

12. Intelligent Stack Widget:
- Make a Smart Stack widget and place it on your main screen. Based on your usage patterns, this widget intelligently presents pertinent information.
Long-pressing on the home screen and choosing the "+" icon will add it.

13. Home Screen Icon Shortcuts:
- Make unique icons for particular activities with the Shortcuts app. To facilitate speedy access to tasks or automation, add these shortcuts to your home screen.

14. Hidden Siri Suggestions Widget:
- For individualized app and shortcut recommendations, add the Siri Suggestions widget to your home screen. Select Siri Suggestions by long-pressing on the home screen and tapping the "+" icon.

15. Personalized Keyboard Shortcuts:
- Make unique keyboard shortcuts for words and phrases you use regularly. To add and configure

shortcuts, navigate to Settings > General > Keyboard > Text Replacement.

16. Custom App Icons:
- To alter app icons, use shortcuts or third-party apps. Some apps provide imaginative ways to replace your app icons, even though Apple doesn't officially support this.

17. Shortcuts to Automate Tasks:
- Check out the Shortcuts app on your iPhone to automate difficult activities. You can download pre-made shortcuts from the Shortcuts Gallery or create unique routines.

18. Customized Ringtones and Vibrations:
- Create unique vibrations and ringtones for each contact. To customize a sound or vibration, edit a contact, touch "Ringtone" or "Text Tone," and select your choice.

19. Emergency SOS Customization:

- Go to Settings > Emergency SOS to customize the Emergency SOS settings. Turn on the "Call with Side Button" and customize the countdown time to suit your needs.

20. Dynamic Backgrounds:
 - Make use of dynamic backgrounds that gradually alter during the day. Select a New Wallpaper > Dynamic under Settings > Wallpaper.

You can completely personalize your iPhone and customize it to suit your own needs and preferences by exploring these advanced settings and customization options. Try different combinations of these settings to see which one improves your overall experience as a user.

CONCLUSION

As we conclude "The iPhone 15: A Comprehensive Guide for Beginners and Experts," it is clear that Apple's most recent iPhone model is the result of combining state-of-the-art technology with a user-centered design aesthetic. With the help of this guide, users new to and experienced alike should be able to fully utilize the capabilities of the iPhone 15, iPhone Pro, and 15 Pro Max by navigating through and customizing them.

For those who were just starting, the process started with learning the basics and completing the necessary procedures to set up the gadget. Users explored third-party apps designed for power users and dug into deeper capabilities as the guide went on. They also discovered hidden shortcuts. It was stressed how software upgrades, security protocols, and accessibility features all work together seamlessly to ensure that consumers are not only skilled at using their iPhones but also knowledgeable about how to keep them secure and operating at peak efficiency.

The thorough investigation of complex settings, modifications, and prospective future trends for the iPhone ecosystem proved valuable to experts. With strategies ranging from using augmented reality to foreseeing foldable designs, the guide sought to offer a forward-looking viewpoint on how mobile technology is changing.

Photography enthusiasts learned how to get the most out of the upgraded camera system, and efficiency-focused users learned how to automate tasks and save time using Siri shortcuts. The focus on customization—both practical and aesthetic—highlighted Apple's dedication to making a product that blends seamlessly with each user's lifestyle.

Since the iPhone 15 series serves a wide range of customers with a variety of demands and interests, the book's comprehensive approach aimed to appeal to a diversified audience. This tutorial aimed to be a go-to resource for anyone looking to maximize productivity, explore the creative potential of the upgraded camera system, or just manage the device with ease.

By the time we finish this guide, you will have seen that the iPhone 15 series represents the pinnacle of design elegance, user experience, and technical advancement. The iPhone ecosystem's ongoing development is a testament to Apple's dedication to giving customers a device that not only satisfies their immediate requirements but also foresees and accommodates emerging trends.

Users of the iPhone 15, iPhone Pro and 15 Pro Max will be at the vanguard of innovation and seamless integration in the rapidly changing world of technology. This handbook unlocks a world of possibilities in the palm of your hand, making it a trustworthy companion whether you are new to using iPhones or an experienced user looking to enhance your skills. I hope the experience you have with your iPhone is as exciting and rewarding as the technology behind it.

www.ingramcontent.com/pod-product-compliance
Lightning Source LLC
LaVergne TN
LVHW051330050326
832903LV00031B/3458